The Fantasy Grayscale Adult Coloring Book

Enchanting Fantasy Fairy Tale Grayscale Coloring

Donald La Due

-Tips-

- Put a piece of thin cardboard between pages when coloring
- Best colored with colored pencils
- Use the dark pens or pencils on the darker shades and the lighter with brighter shades
- Watercolors and other wet media are not recommended

Enjoy!

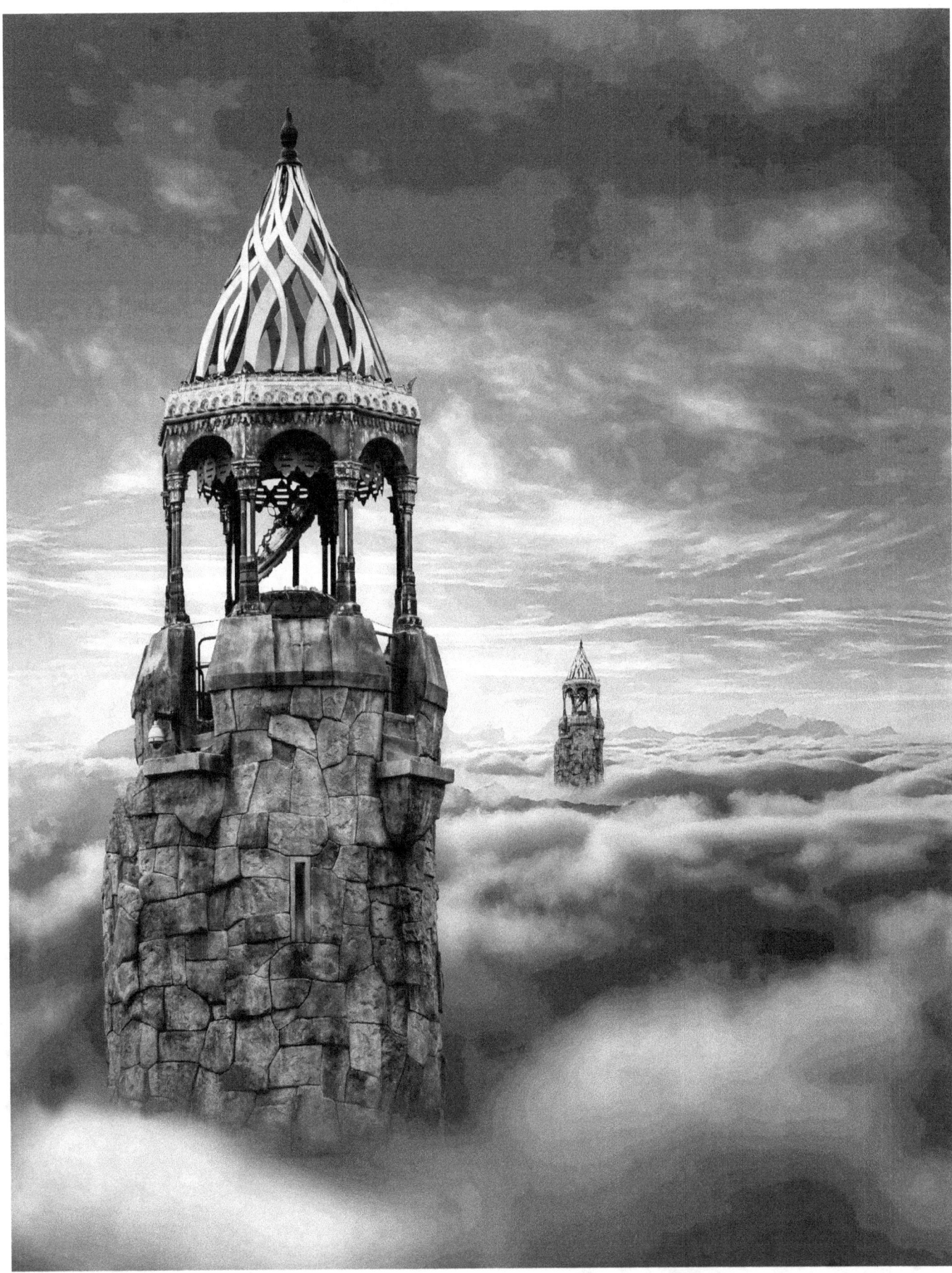

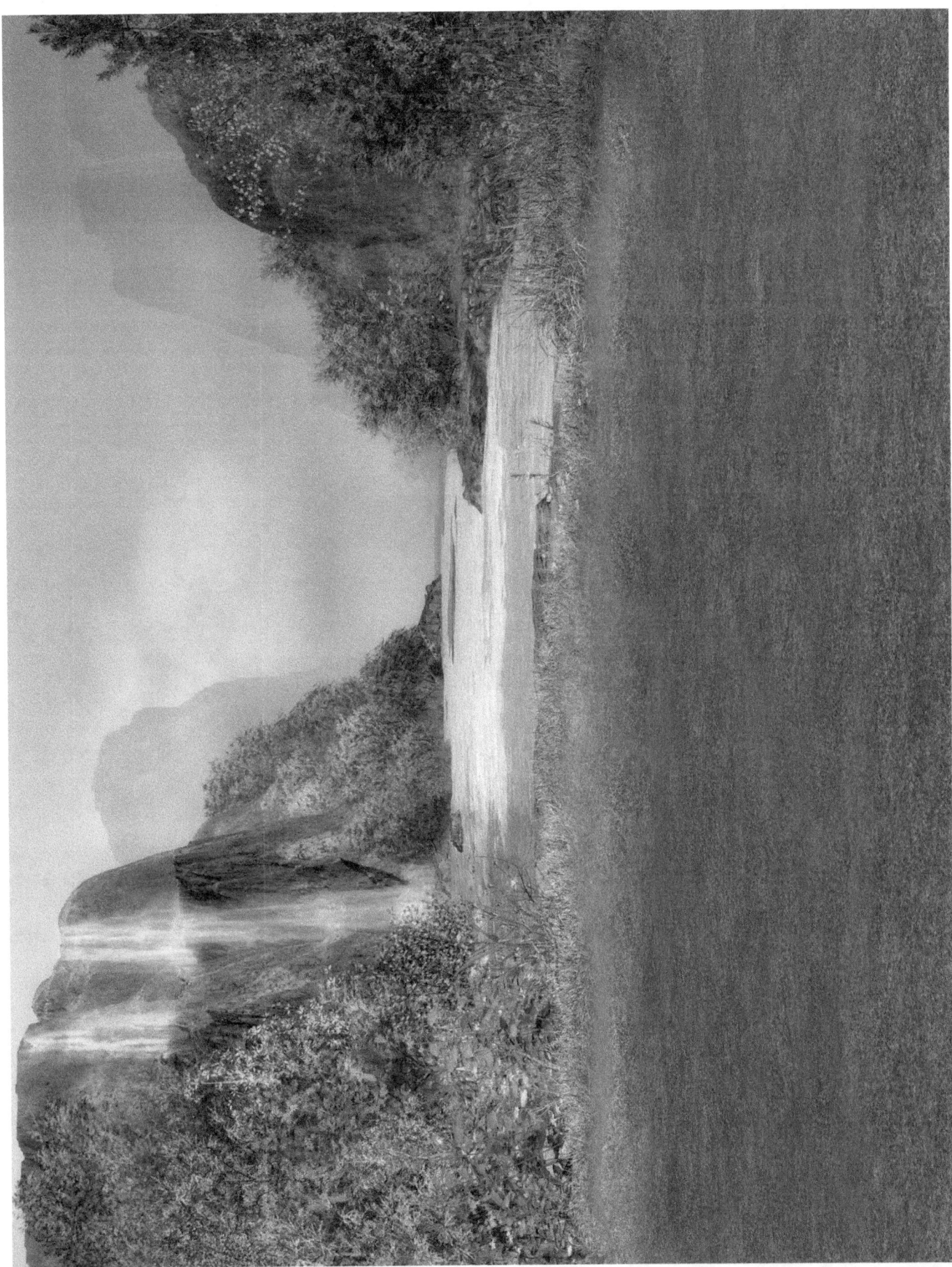

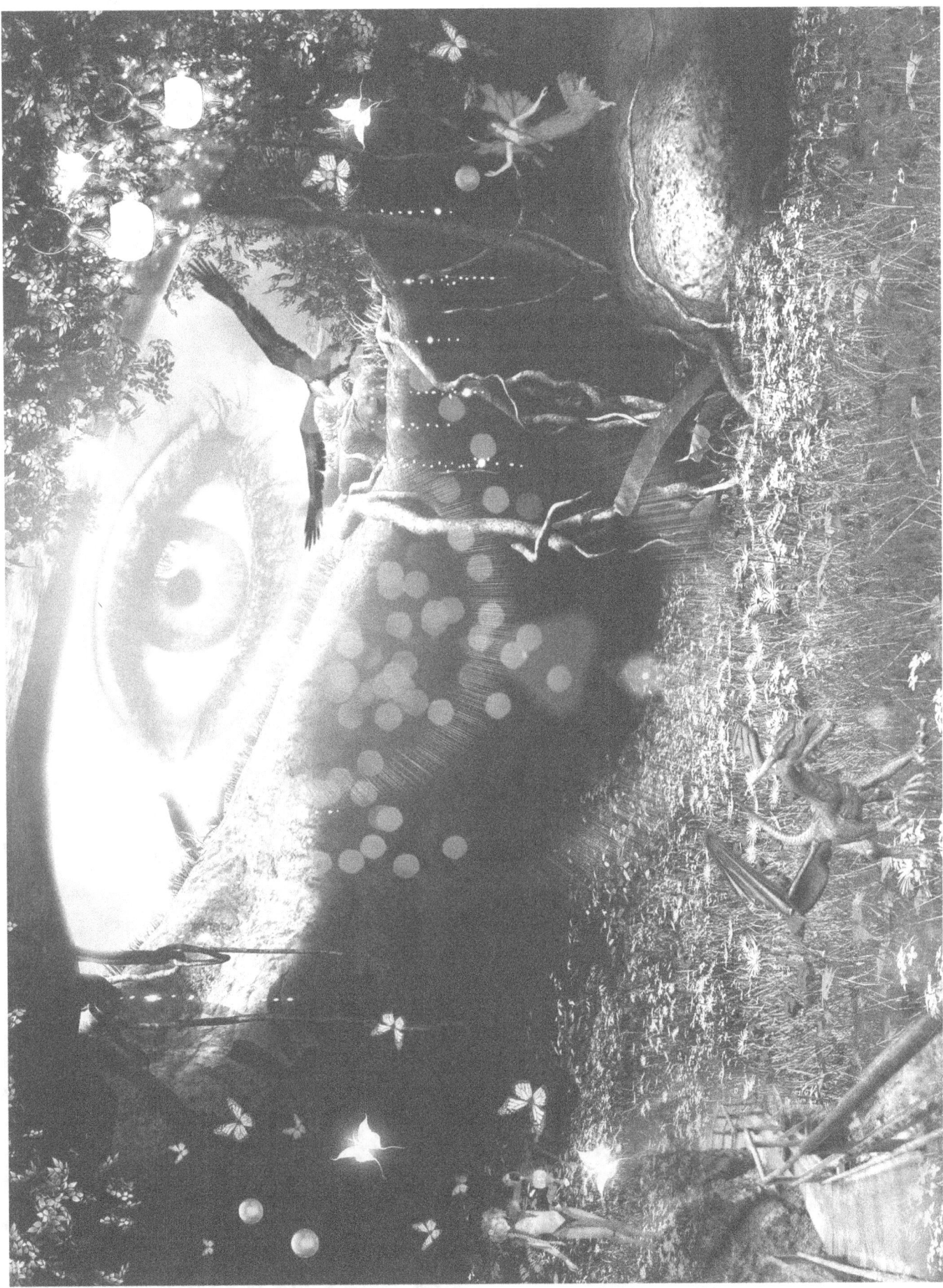

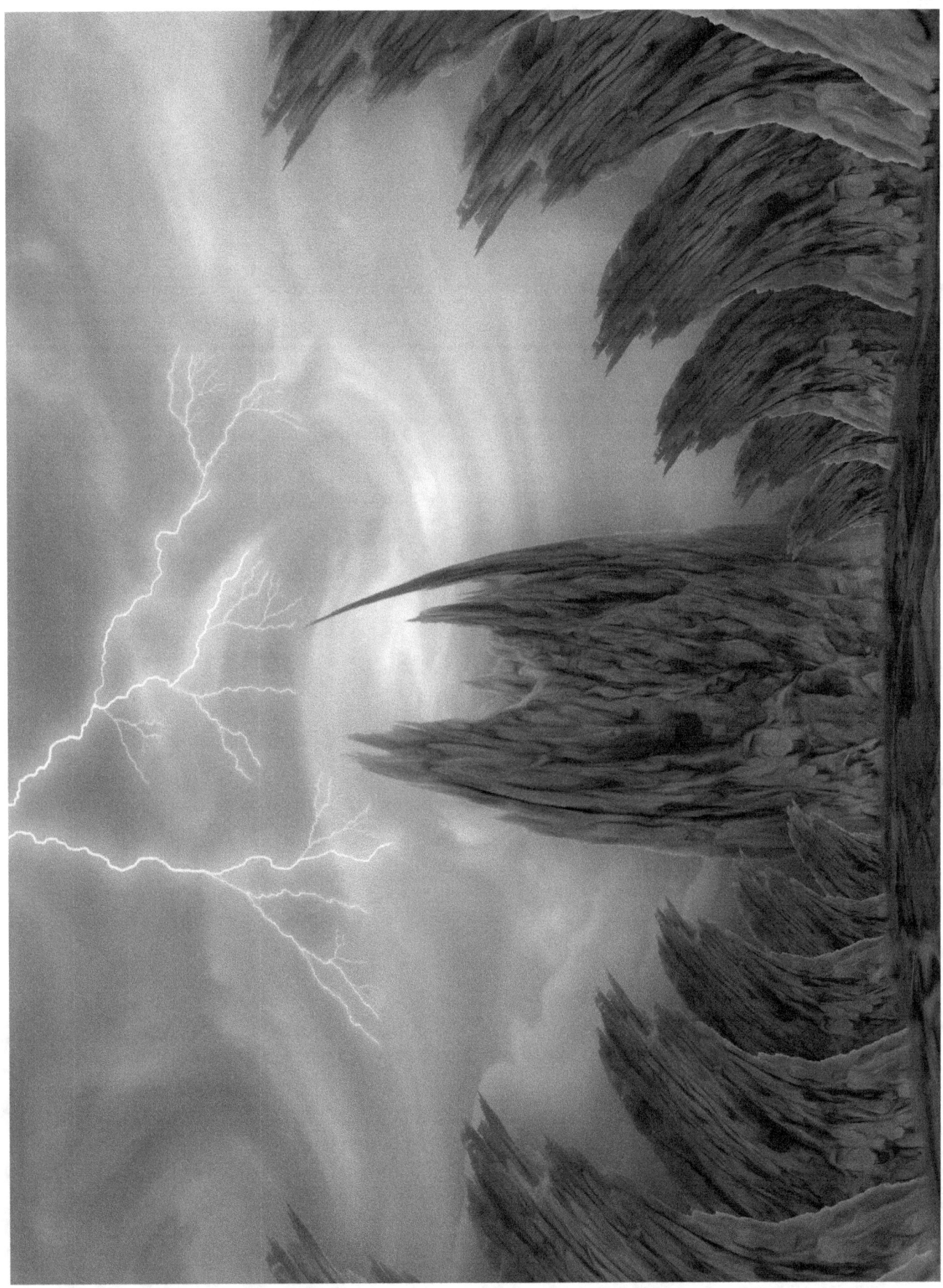

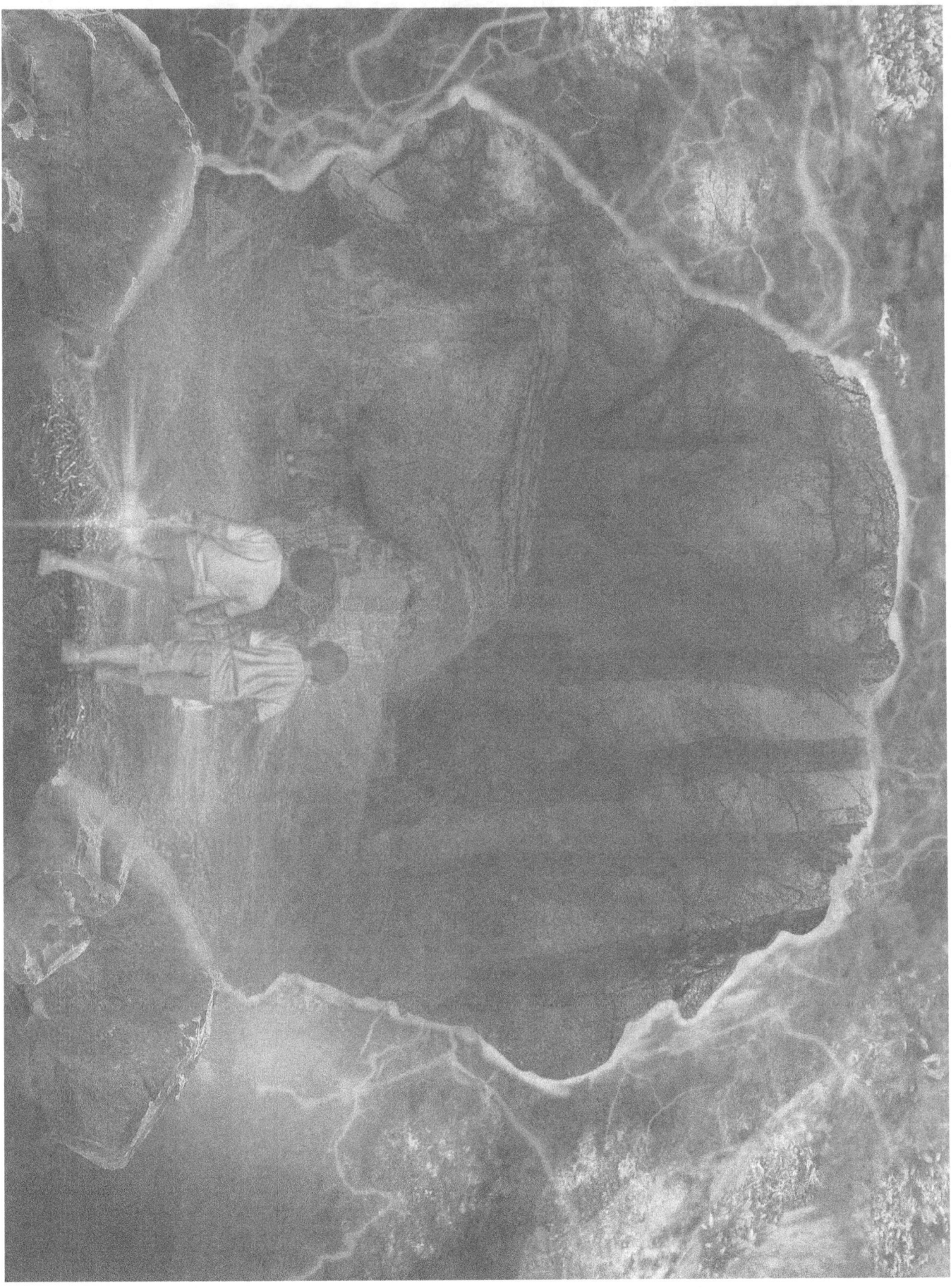

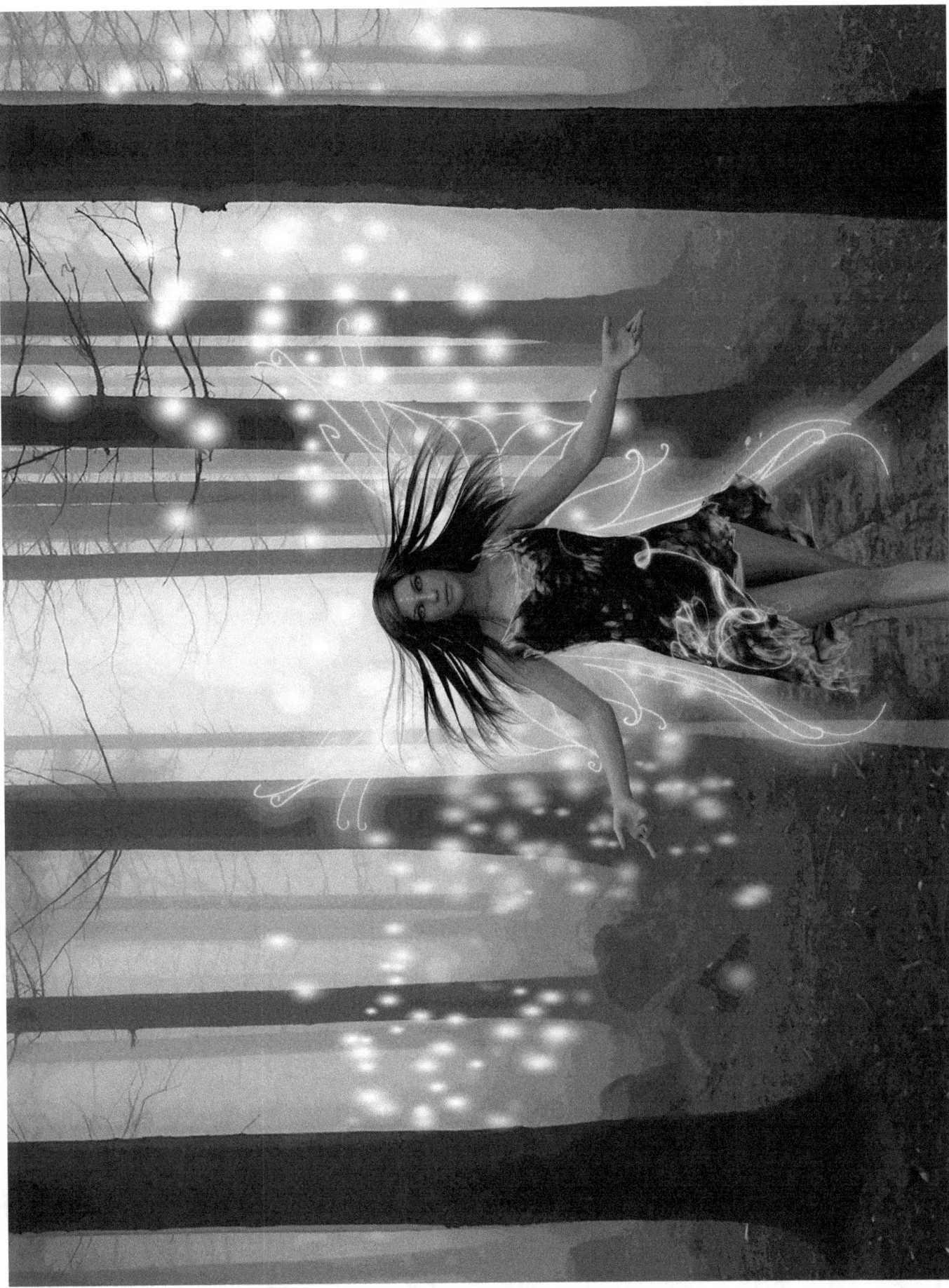

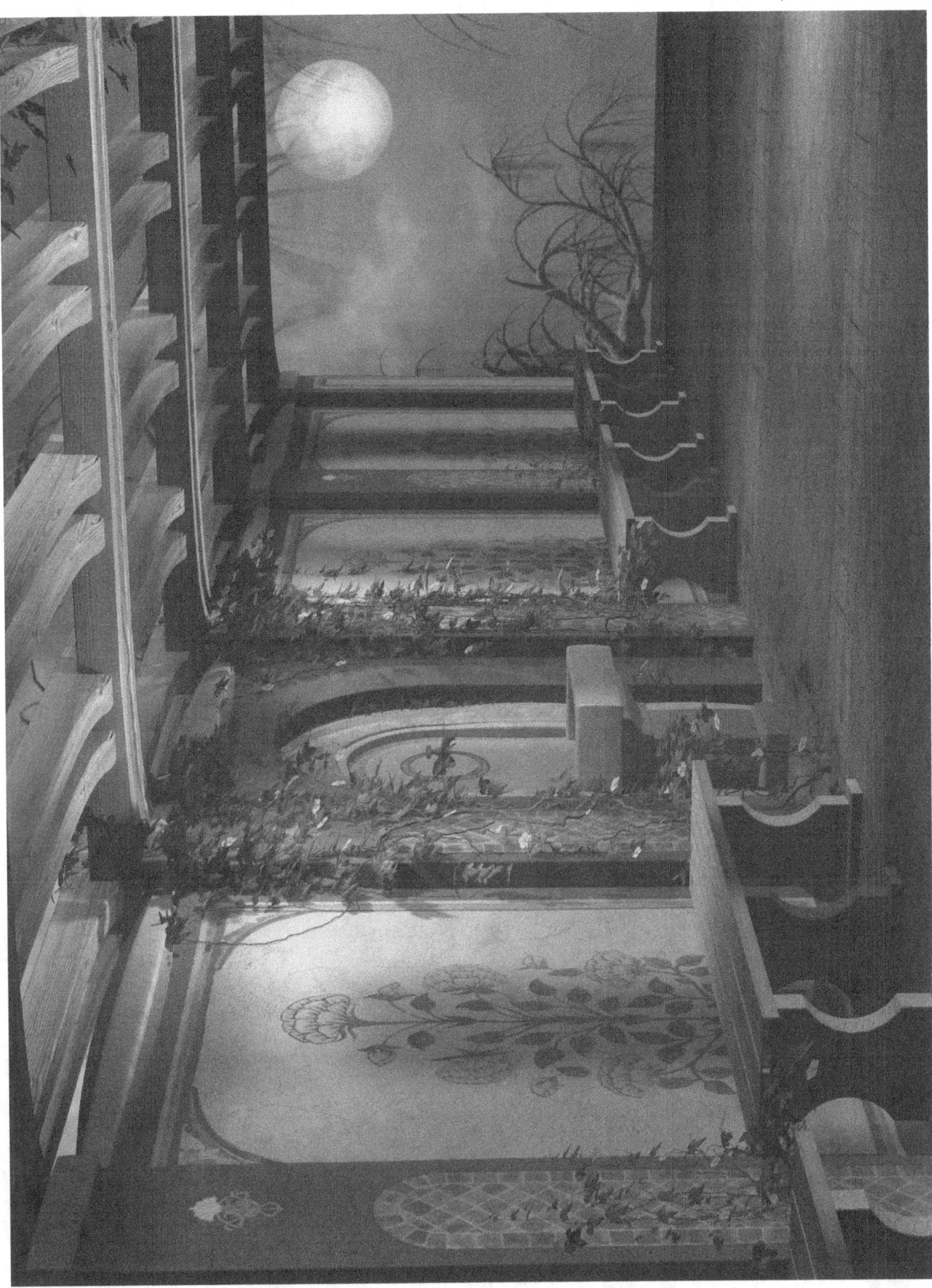

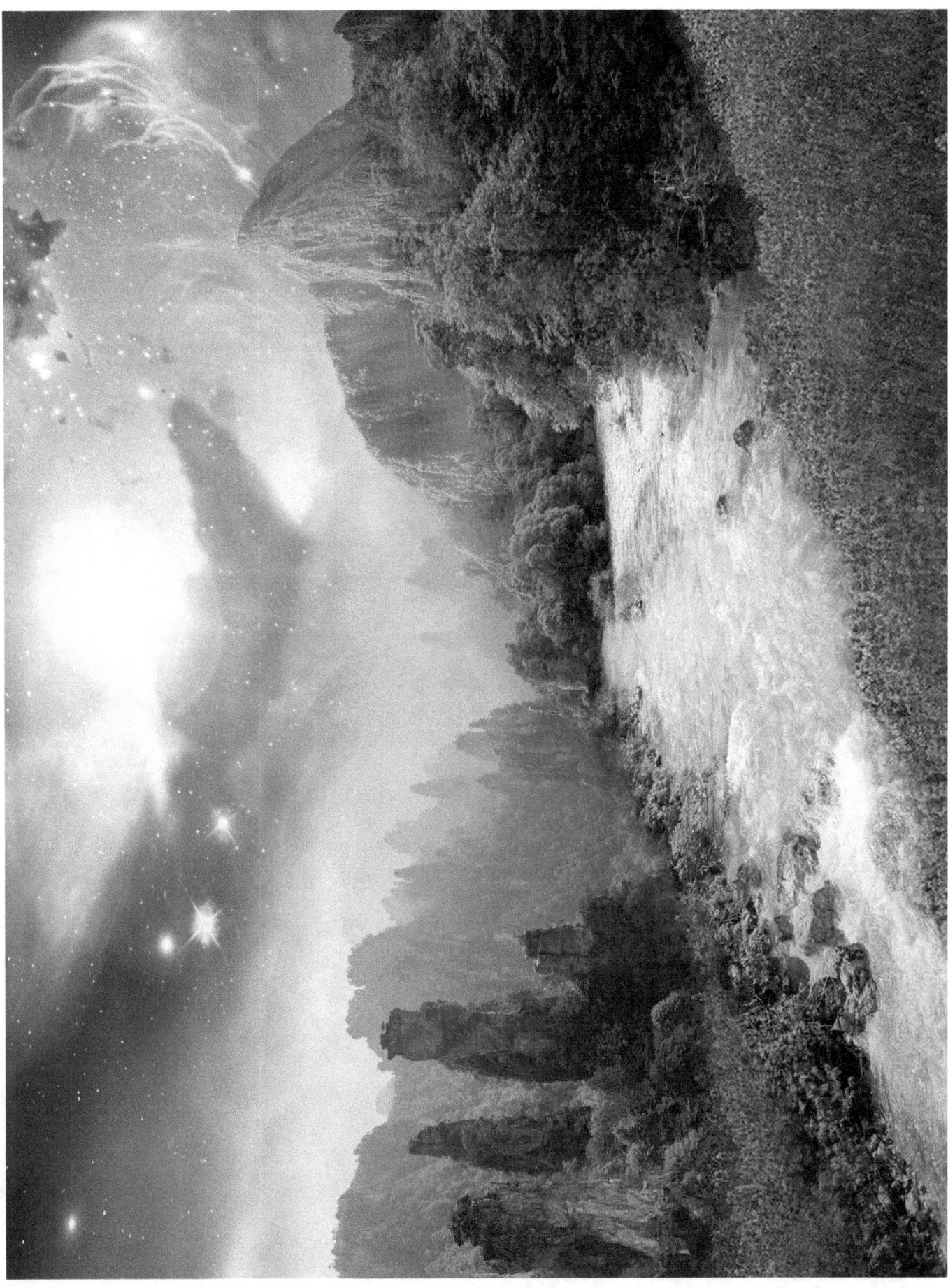

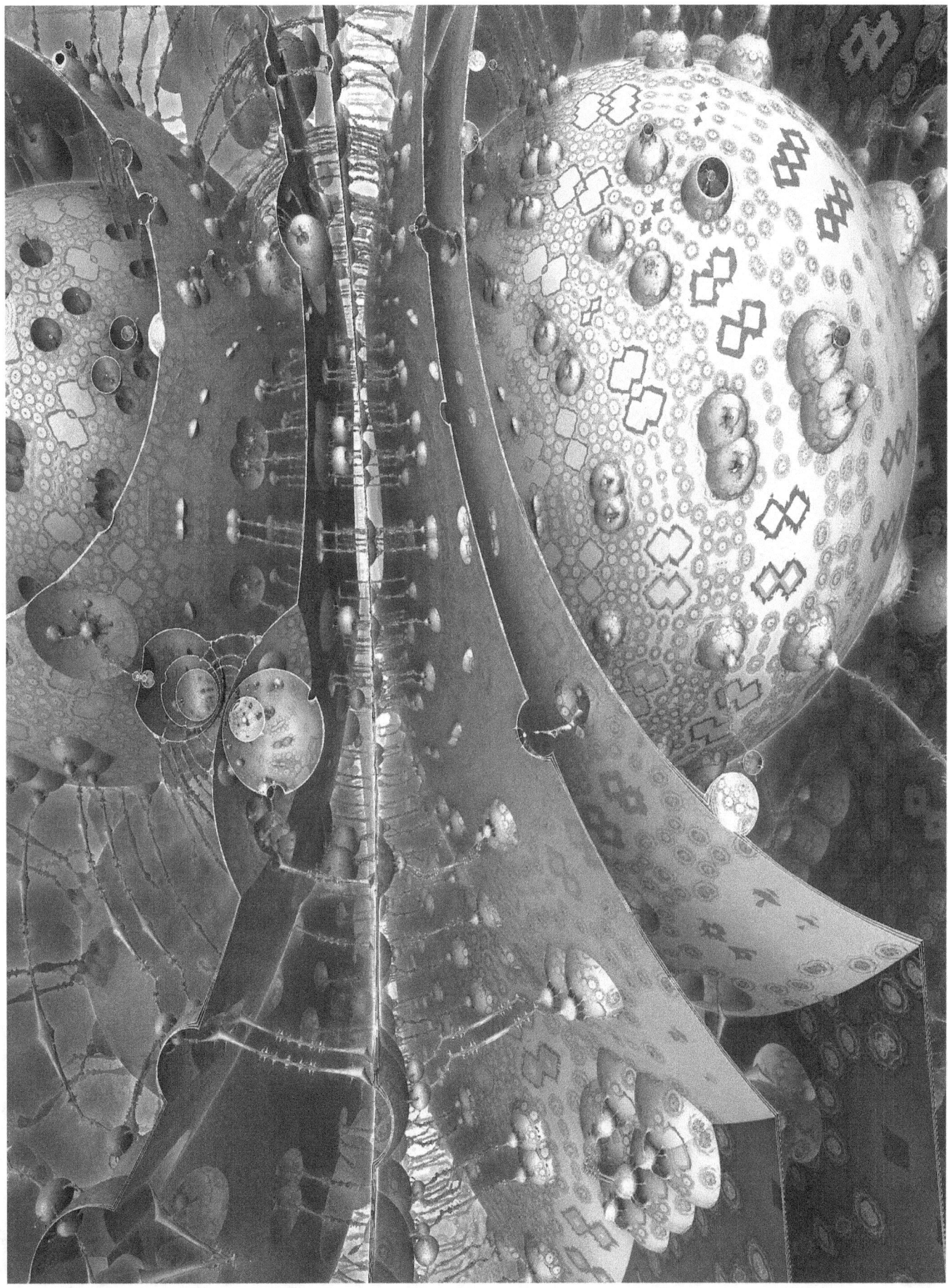

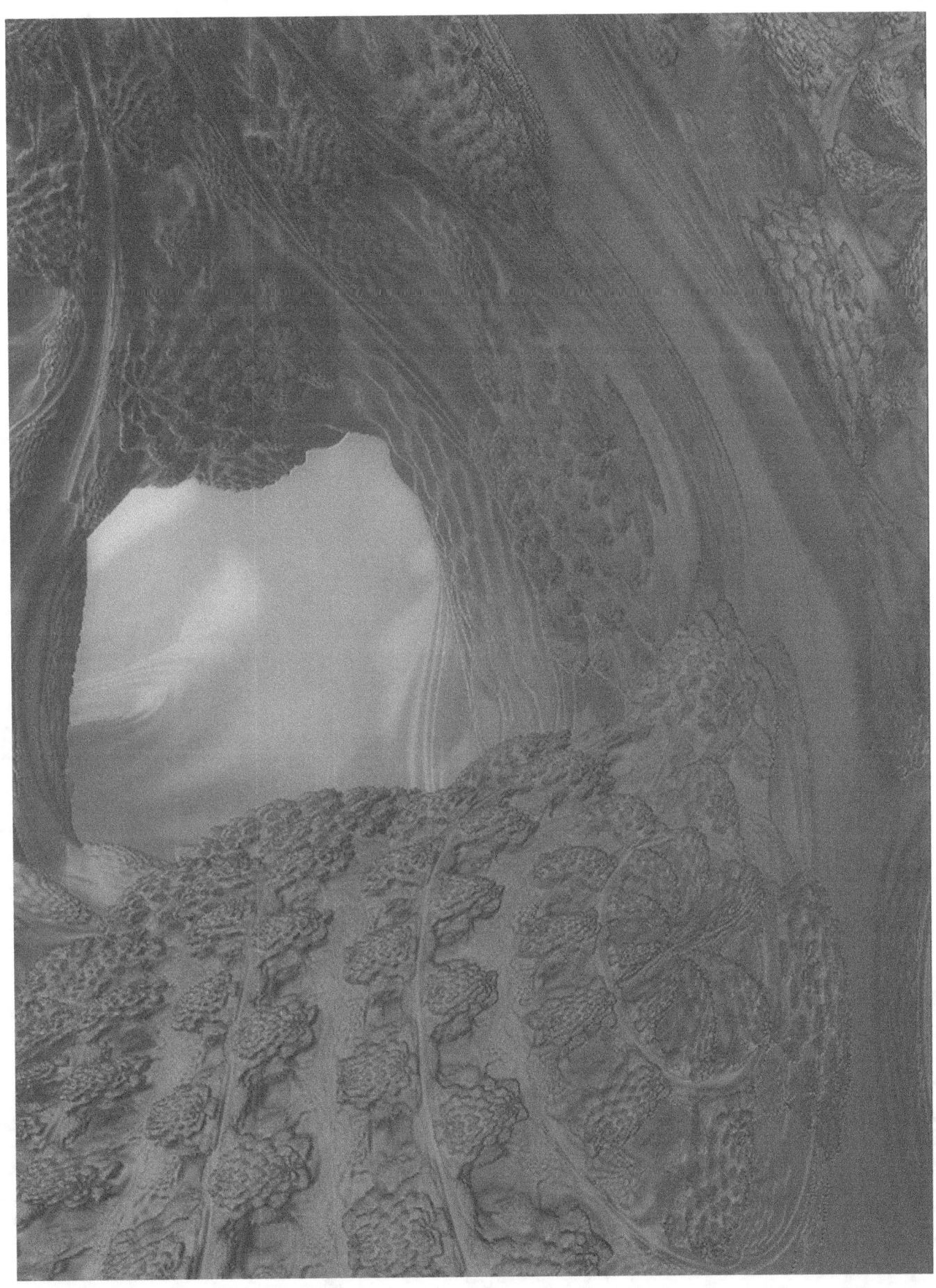

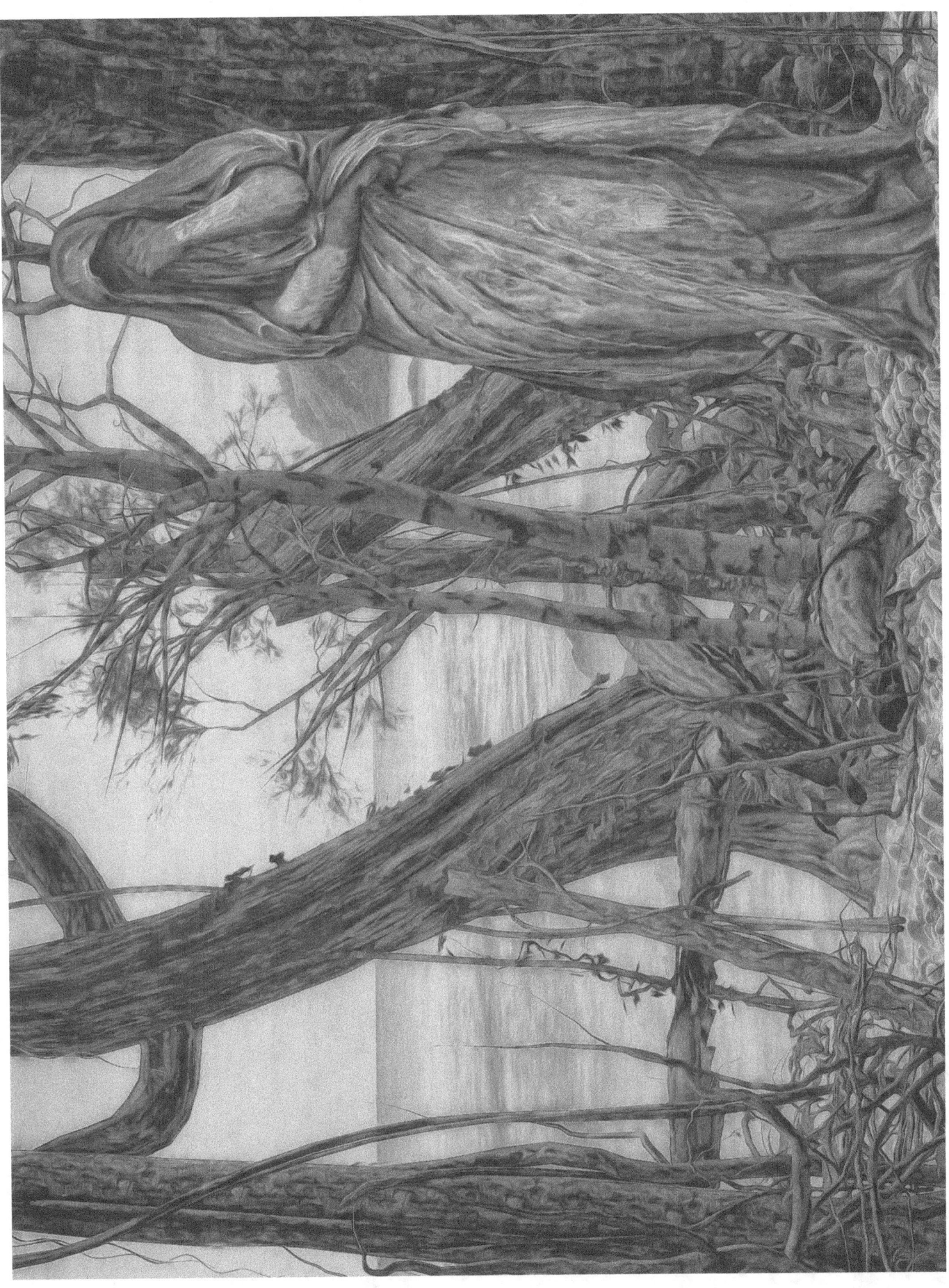

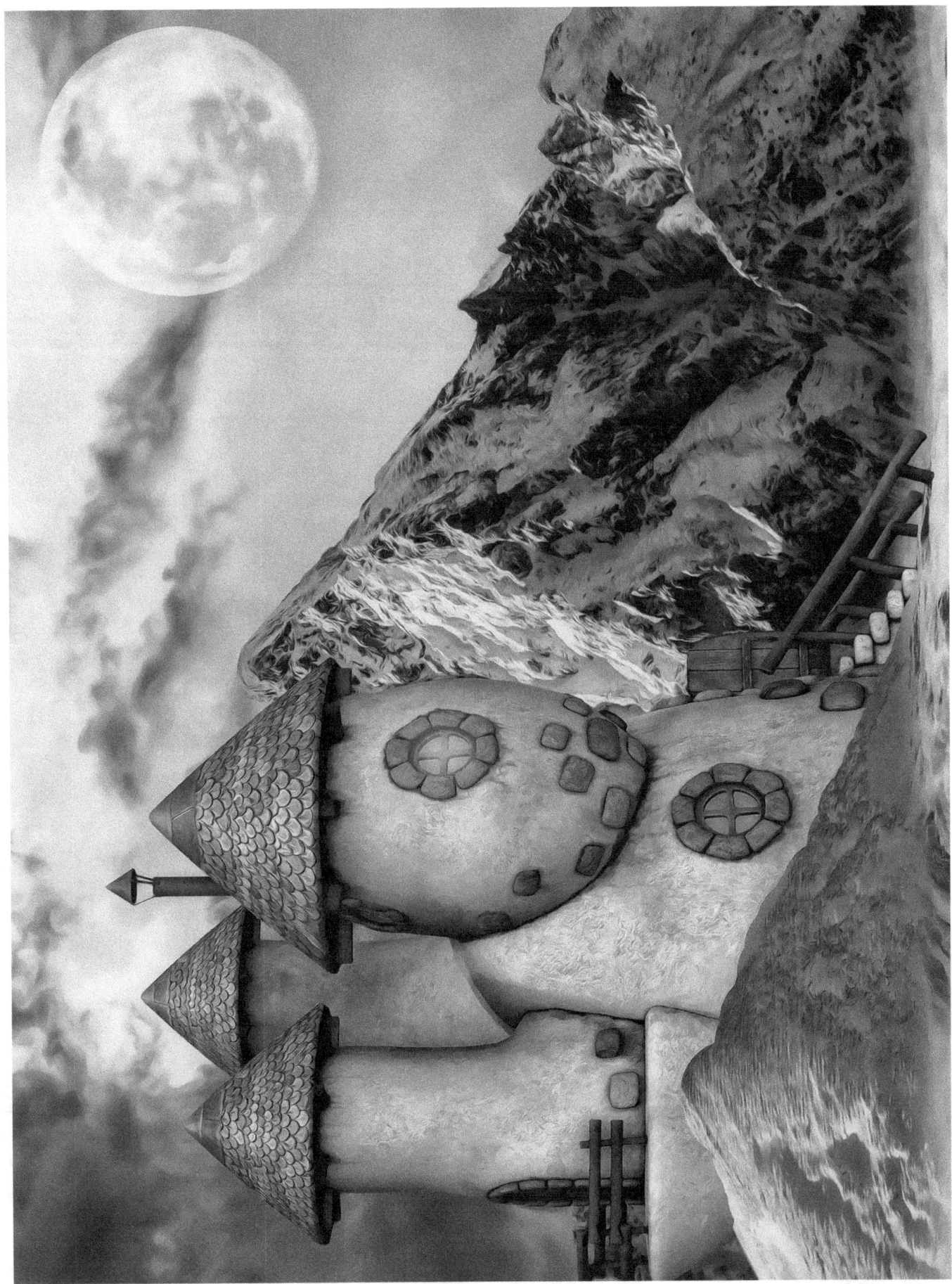

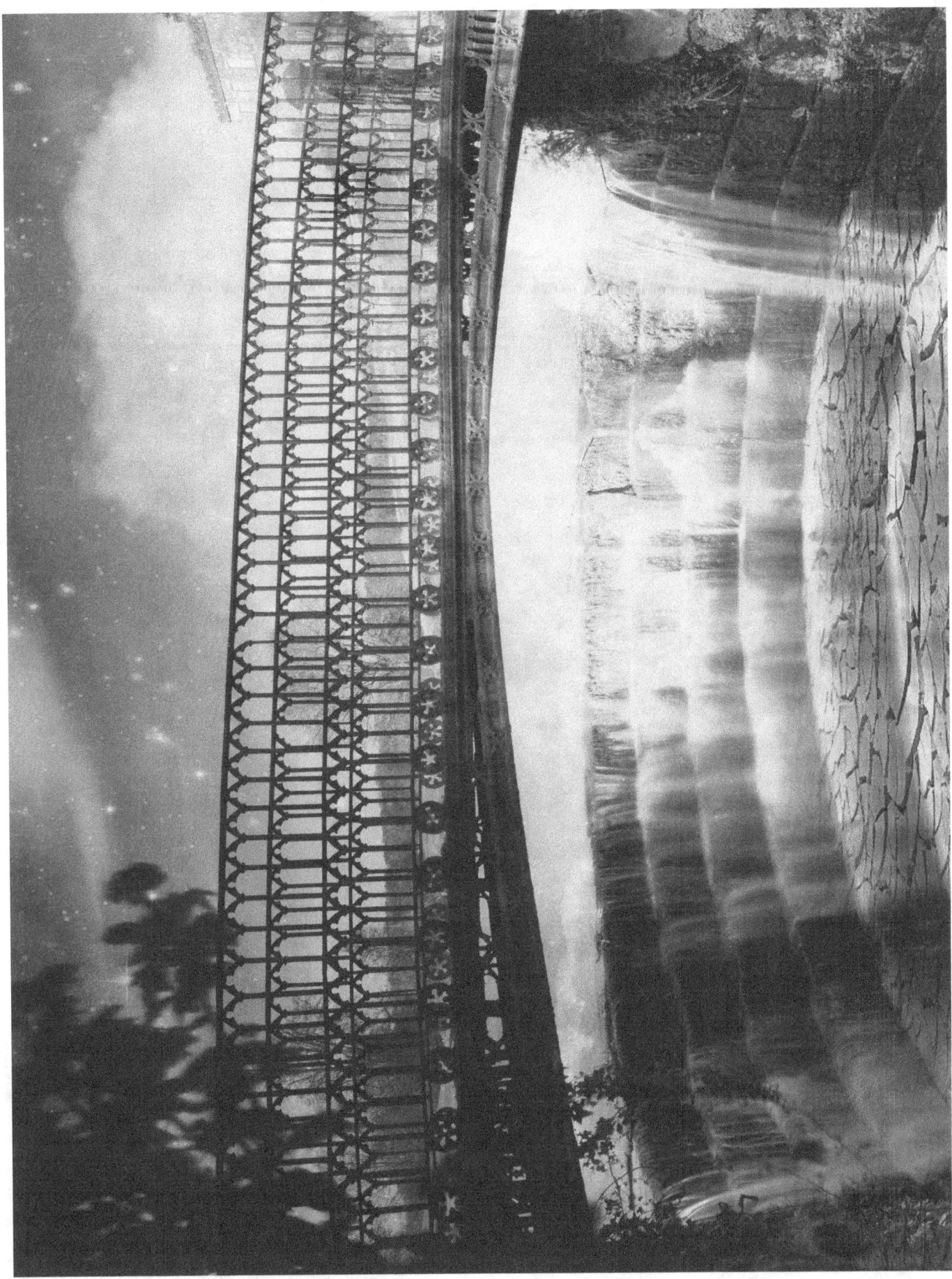

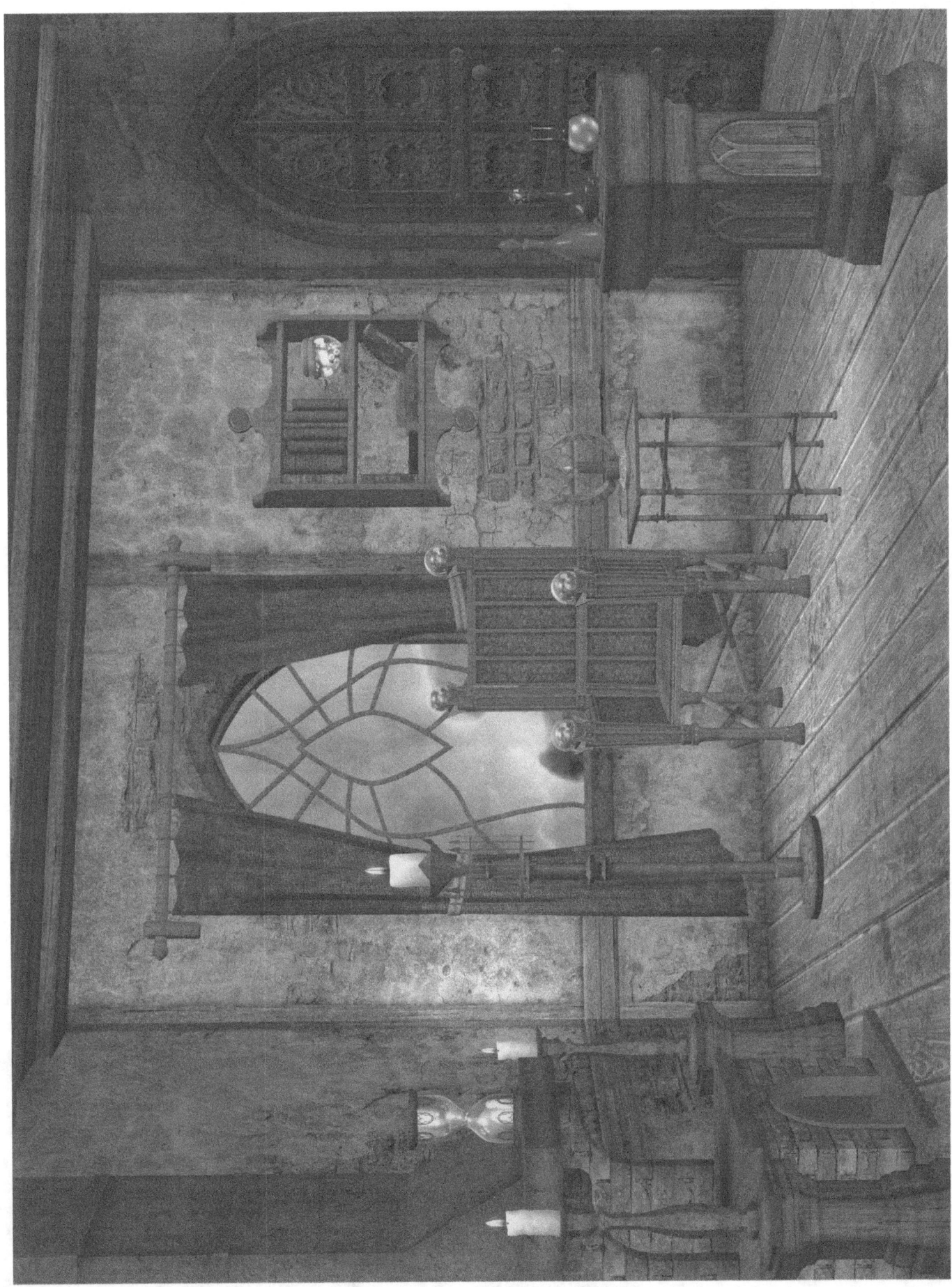

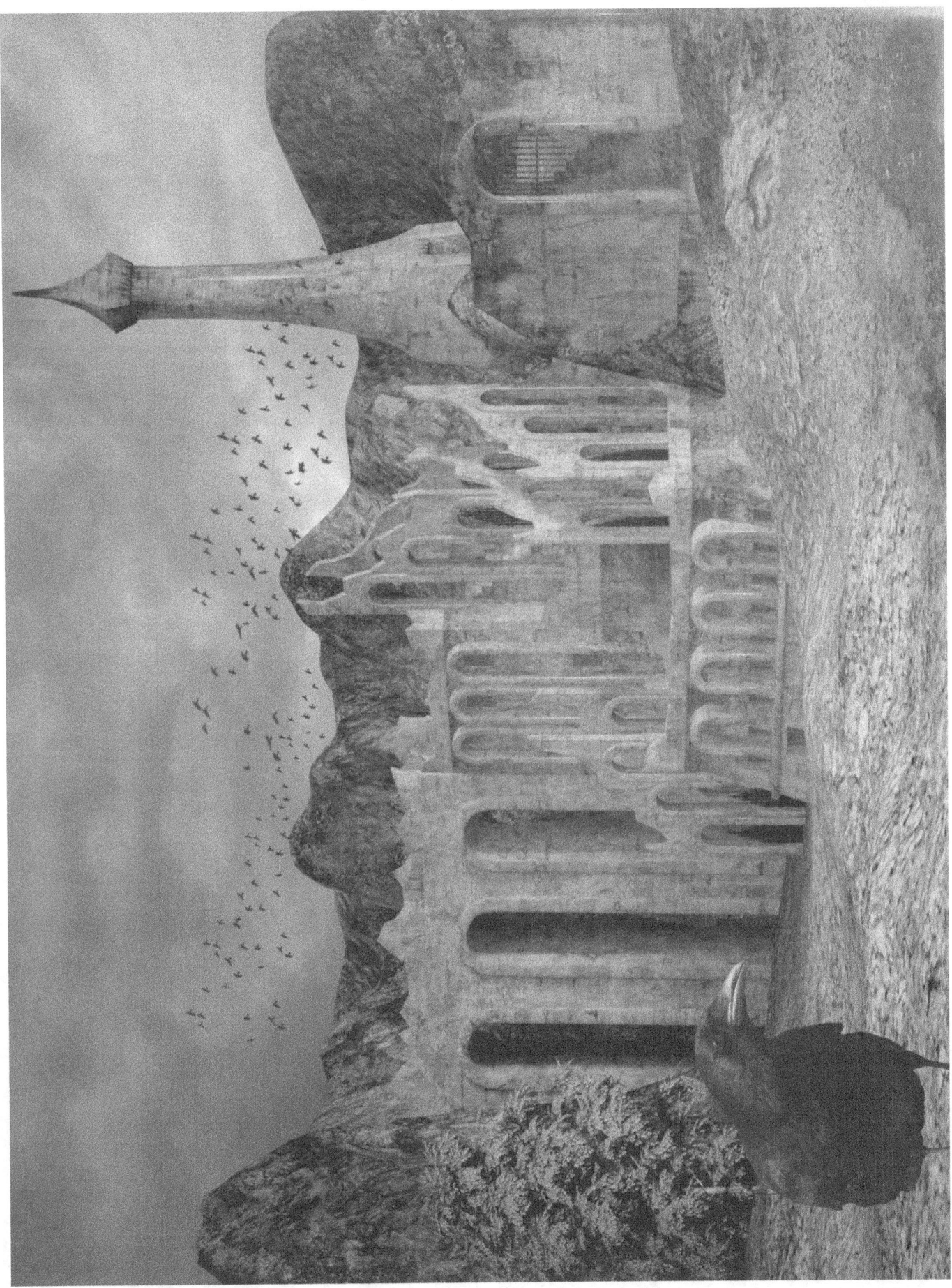

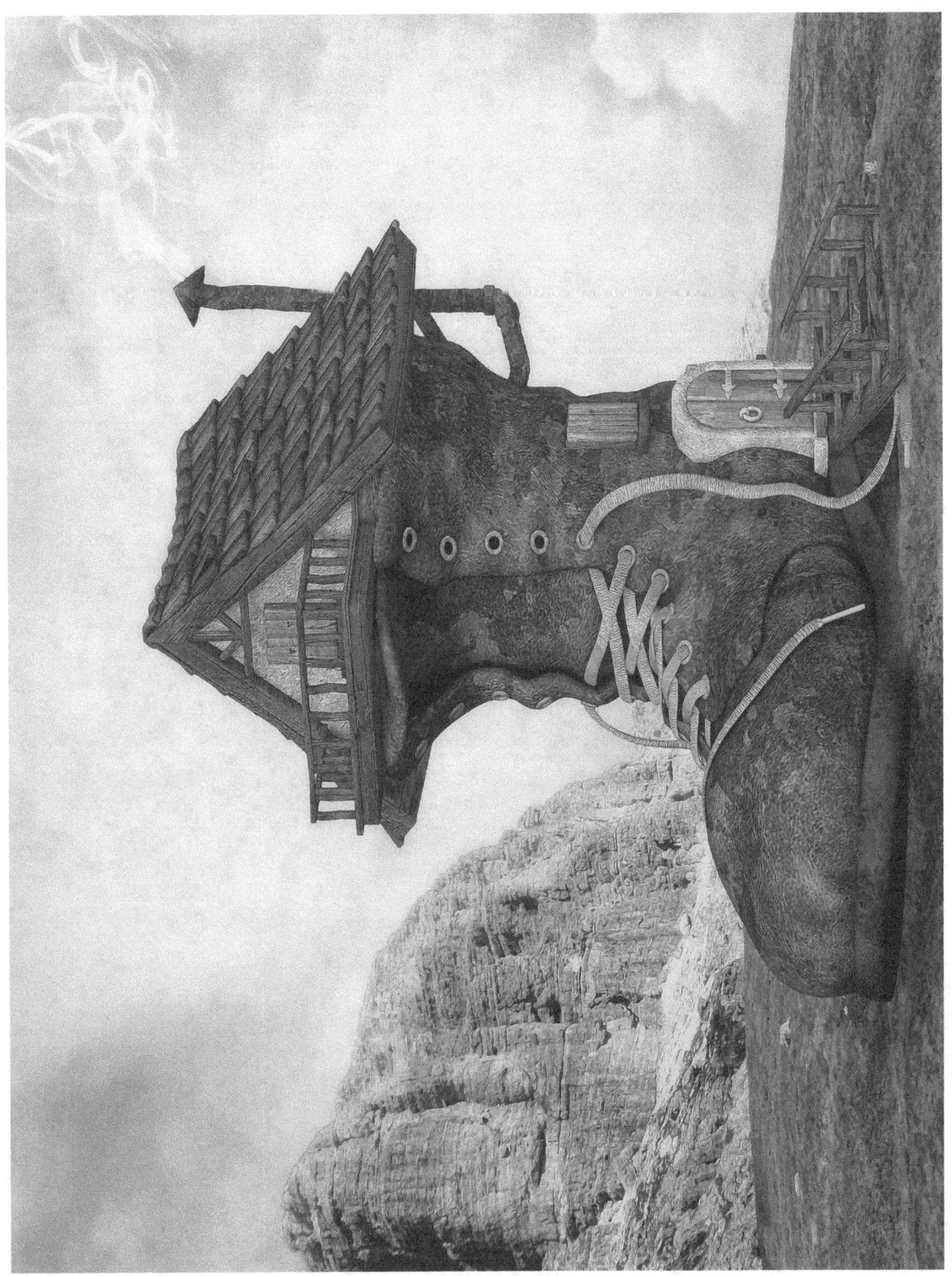

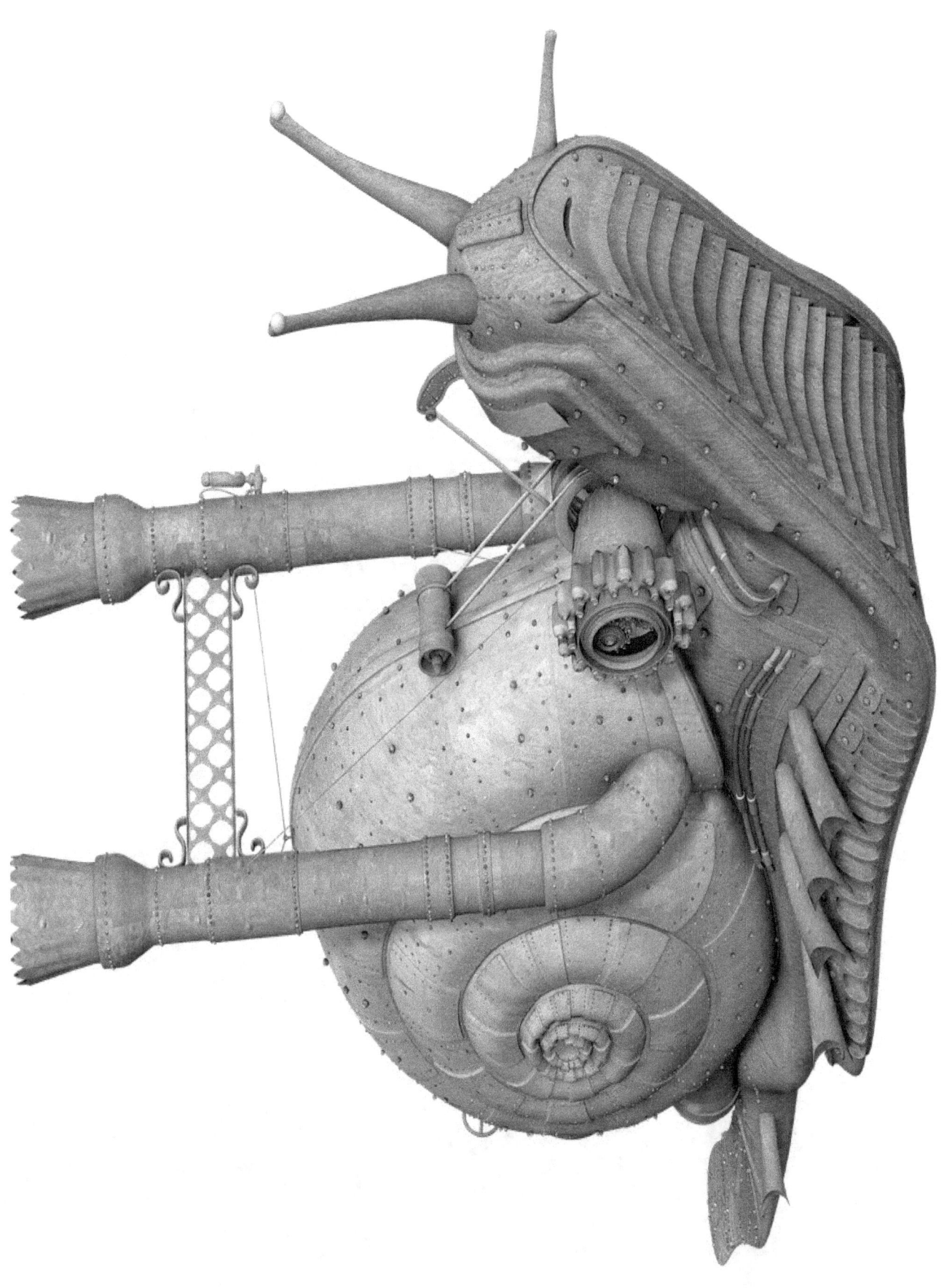

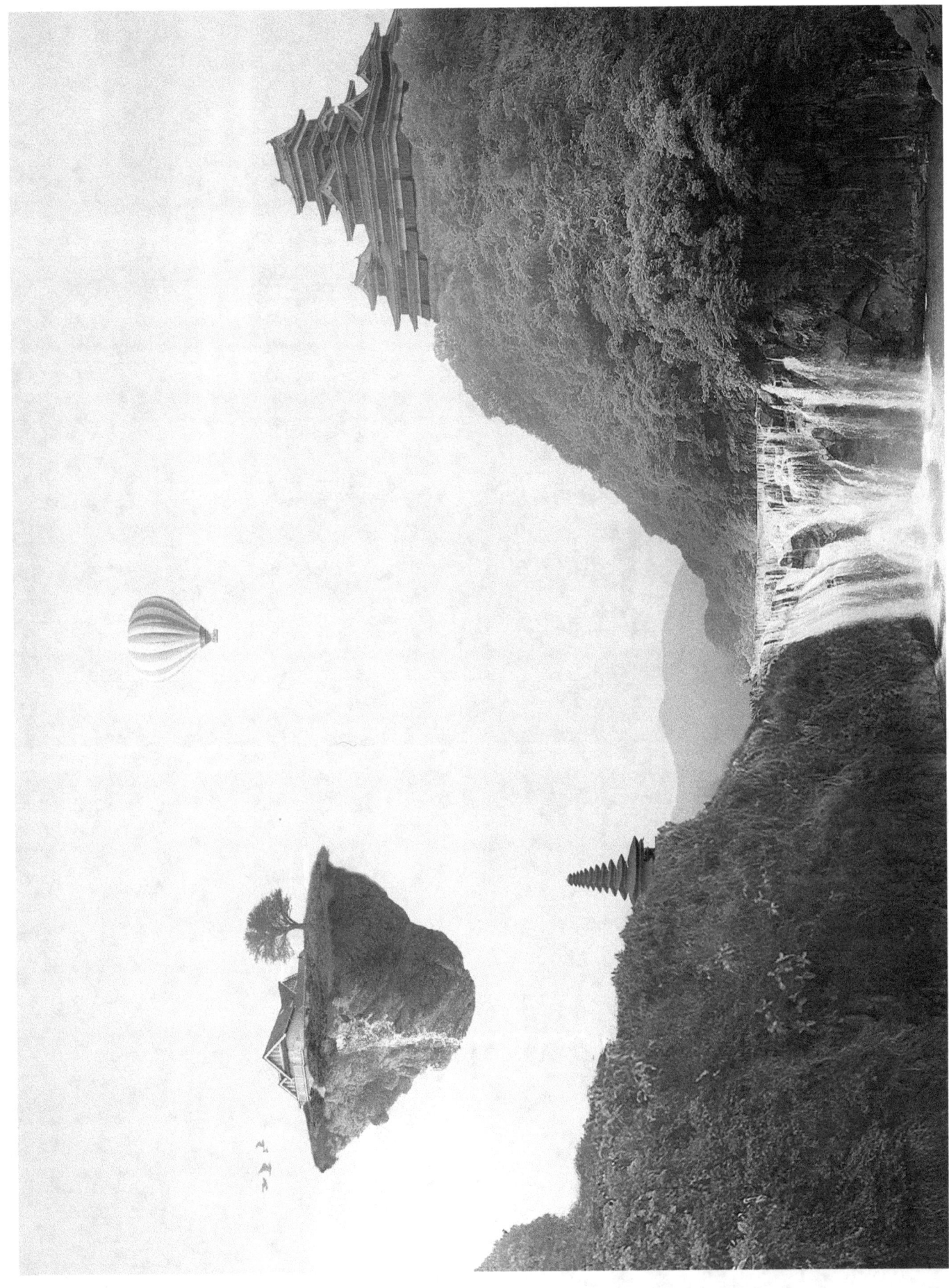

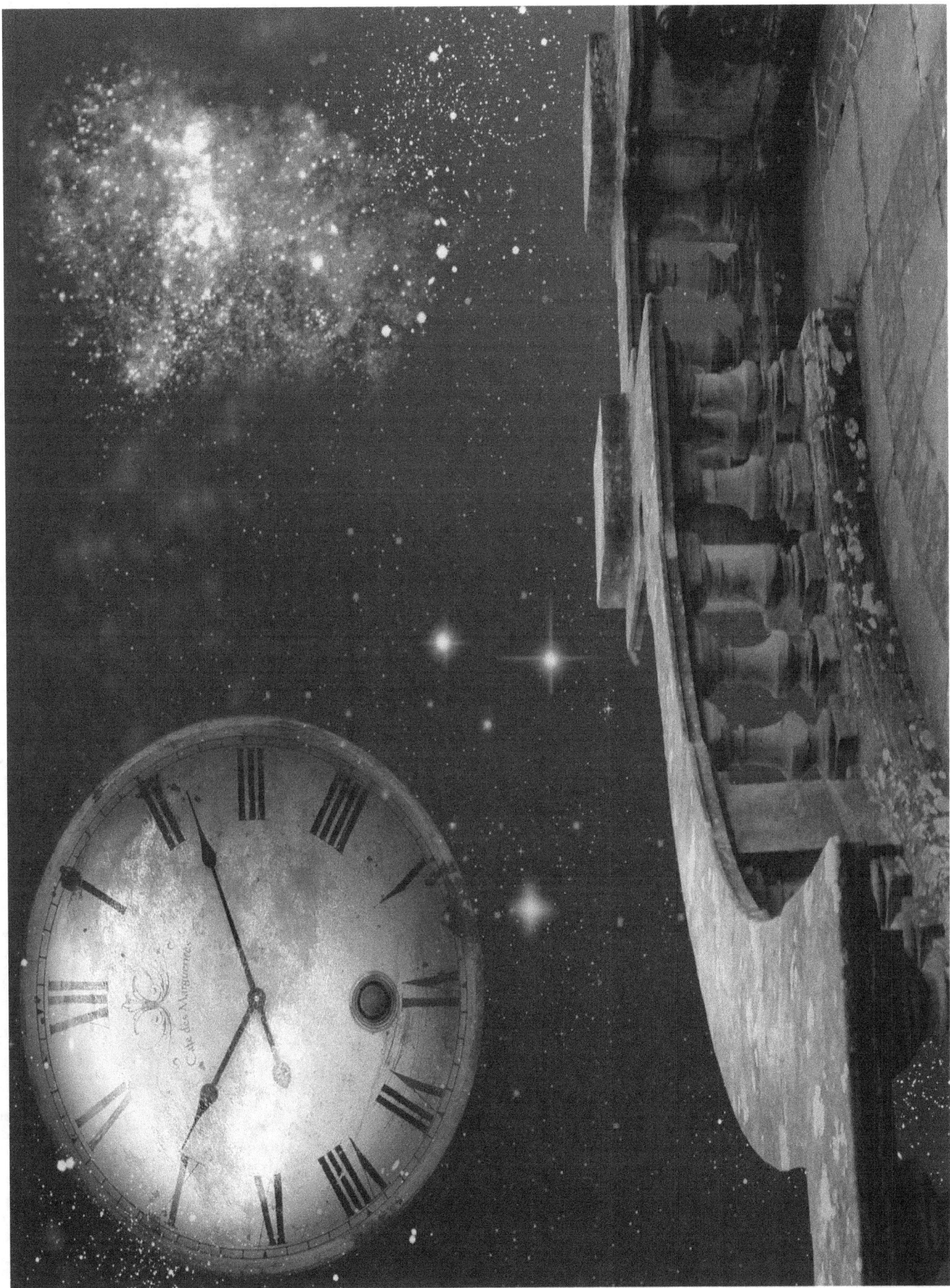

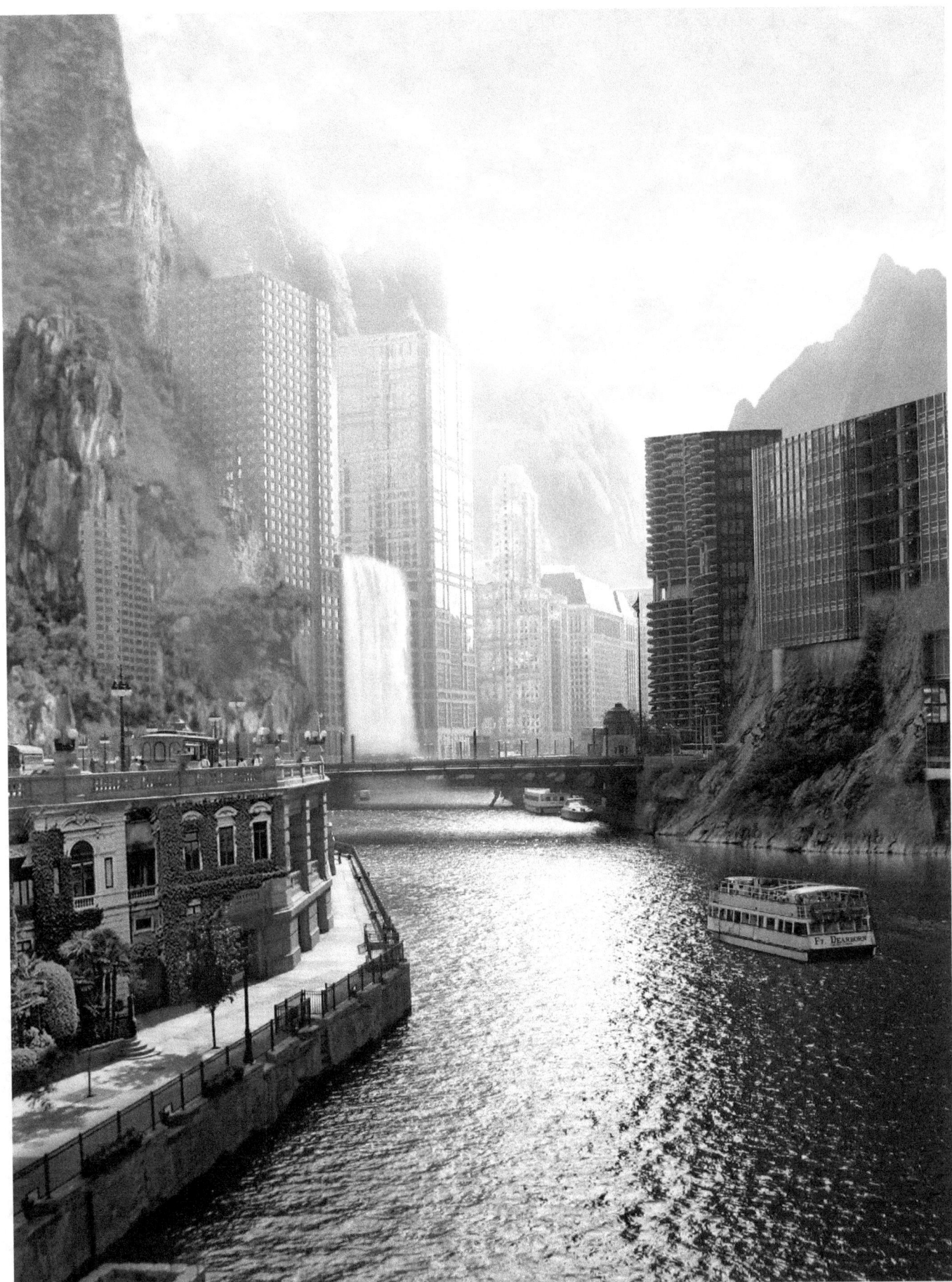

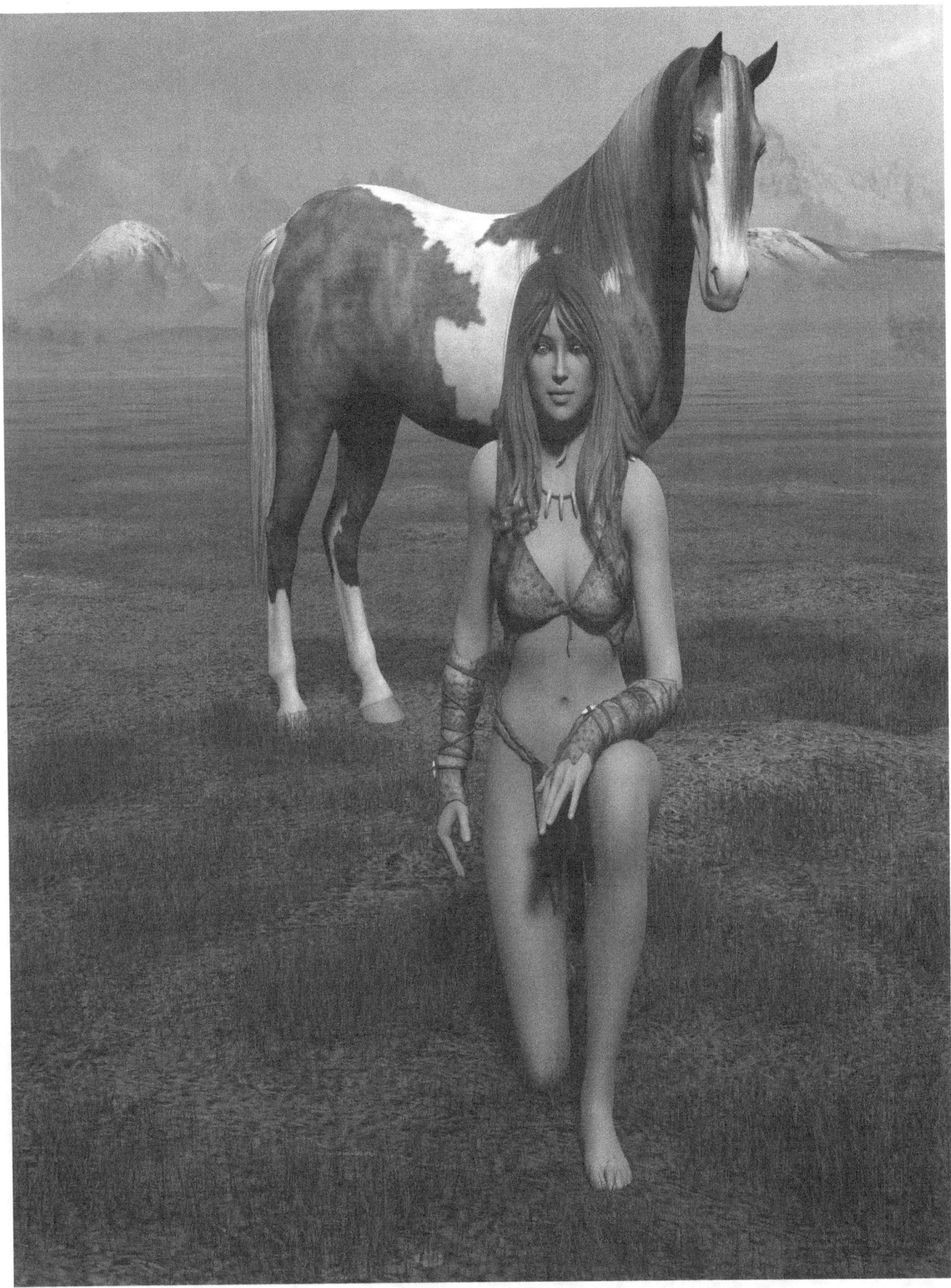

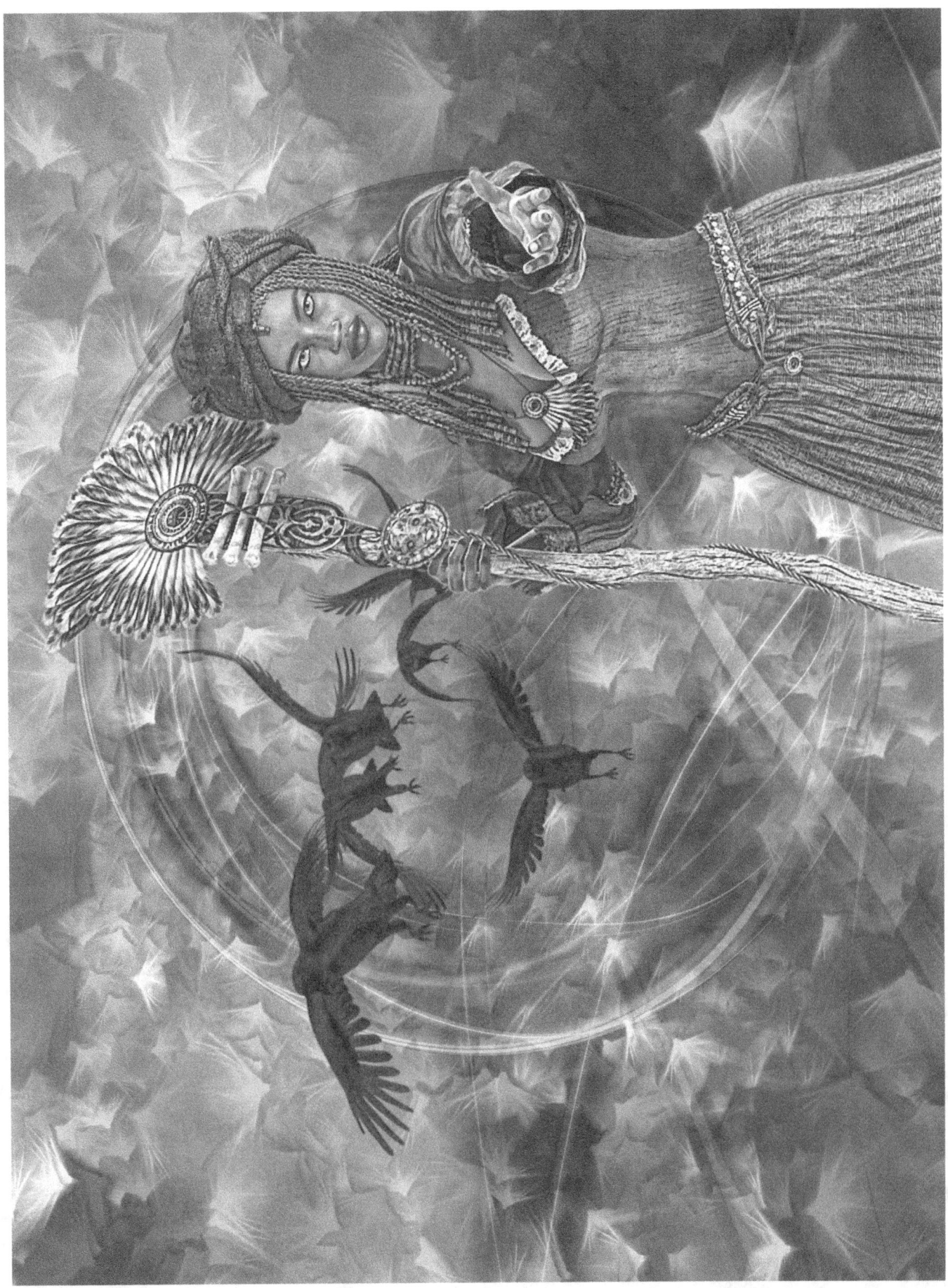

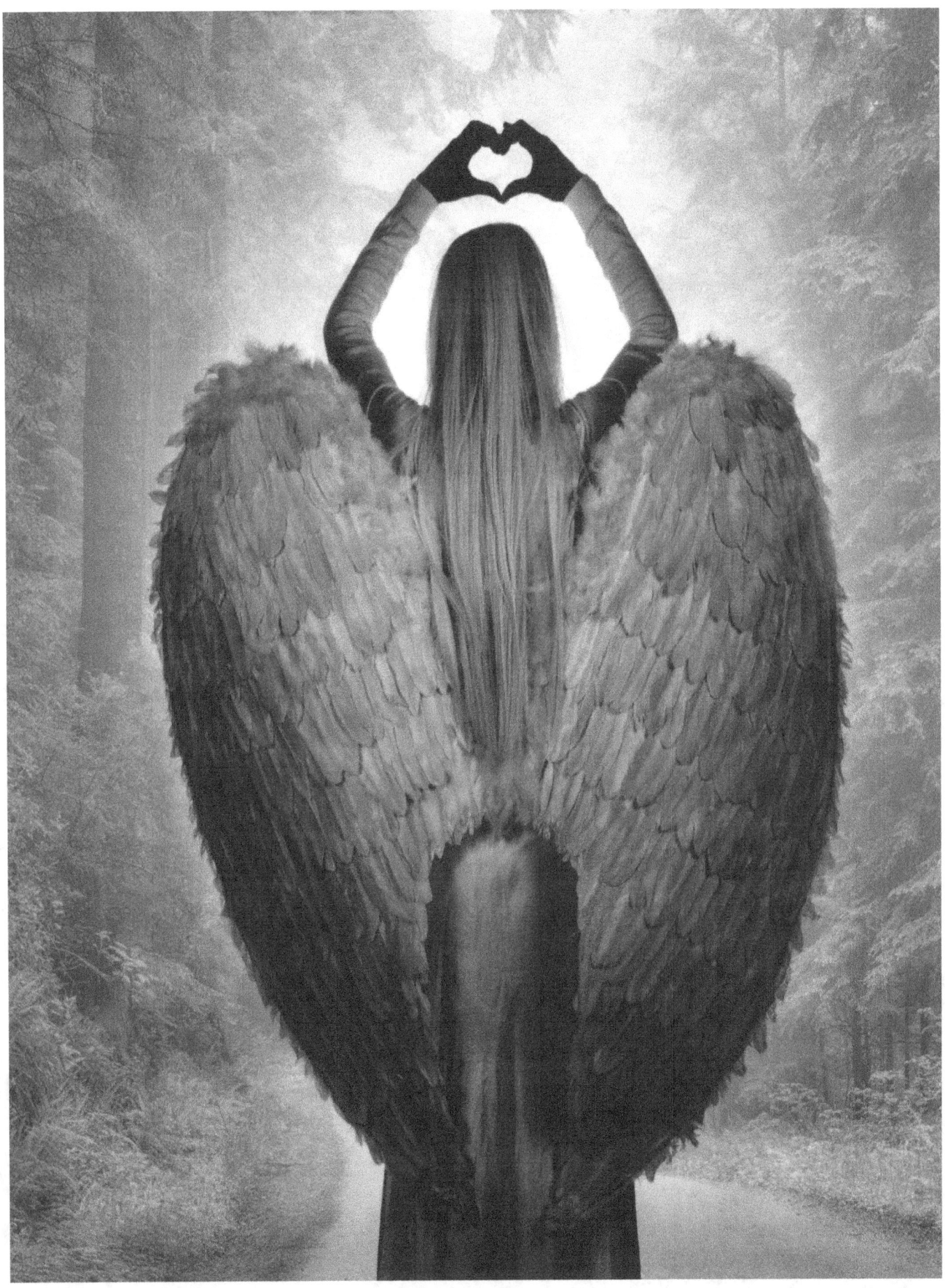

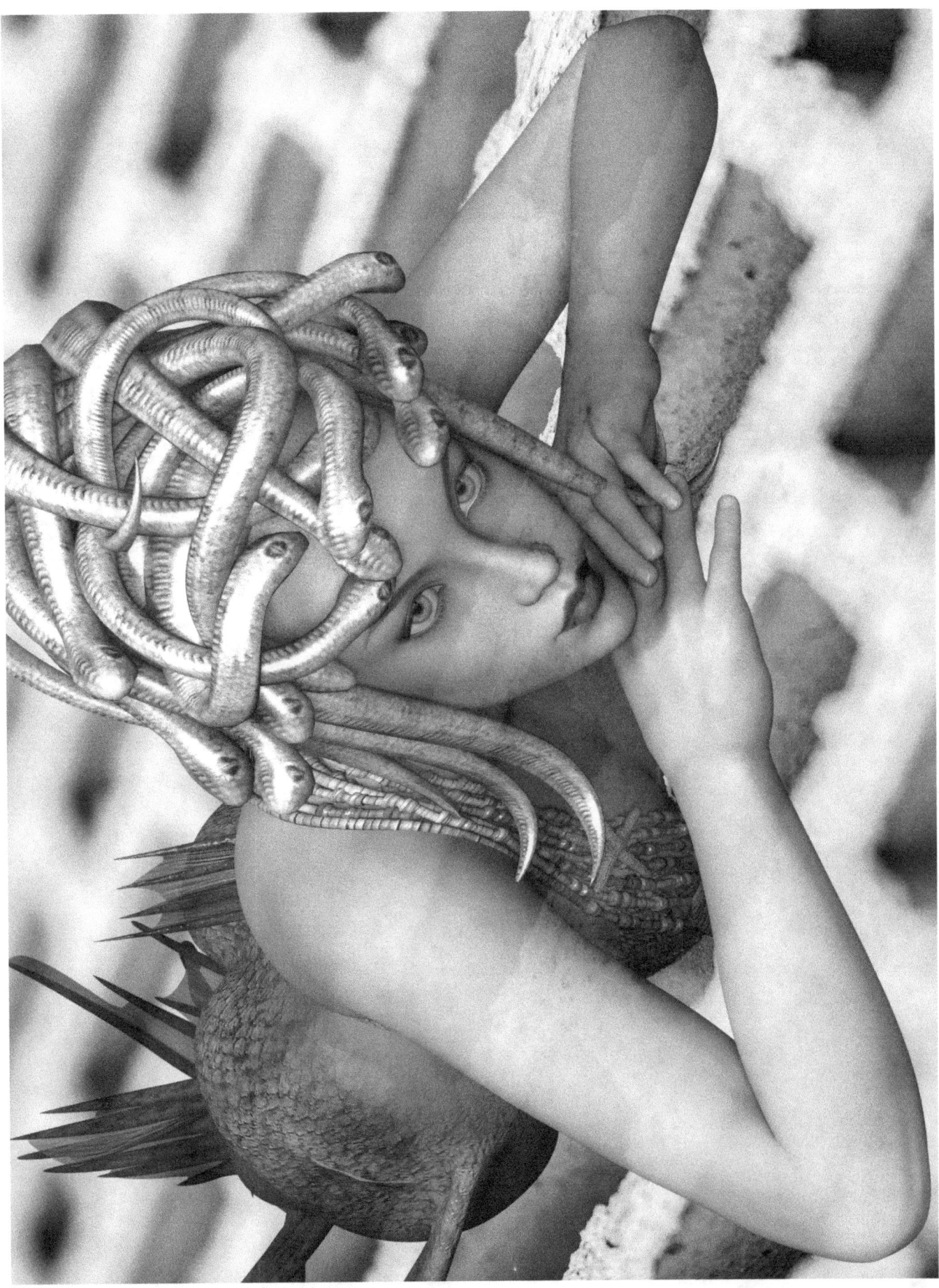

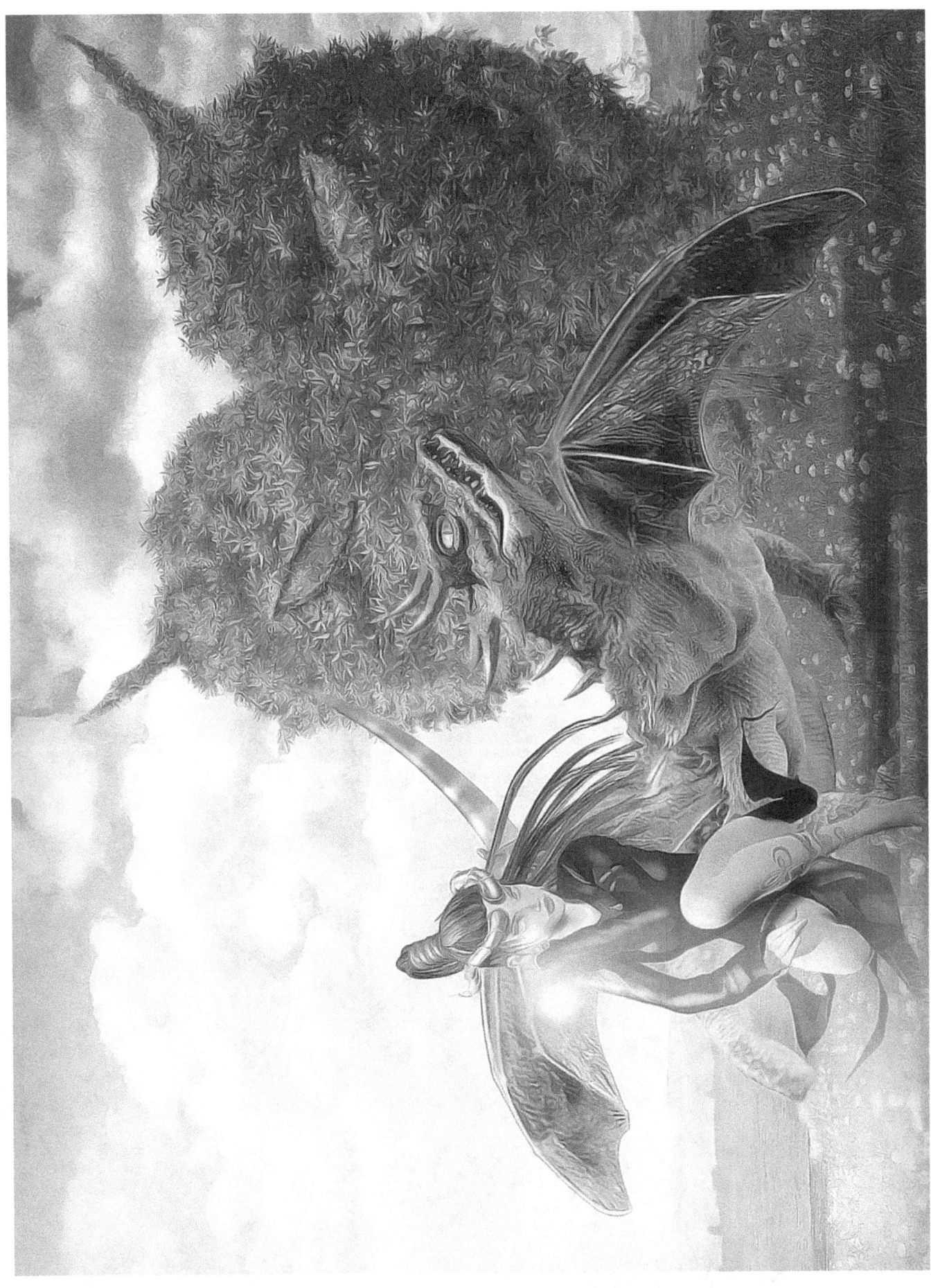

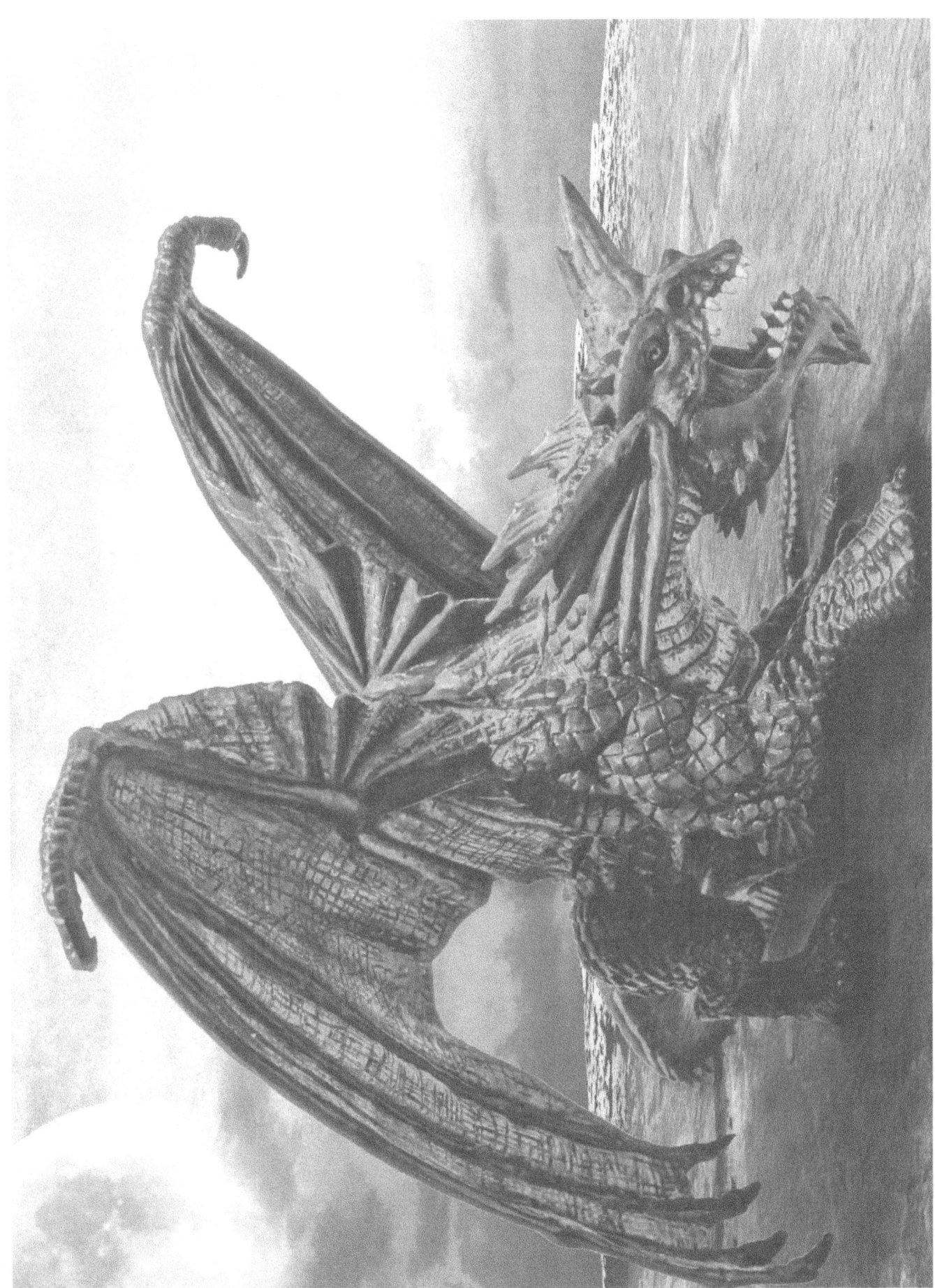

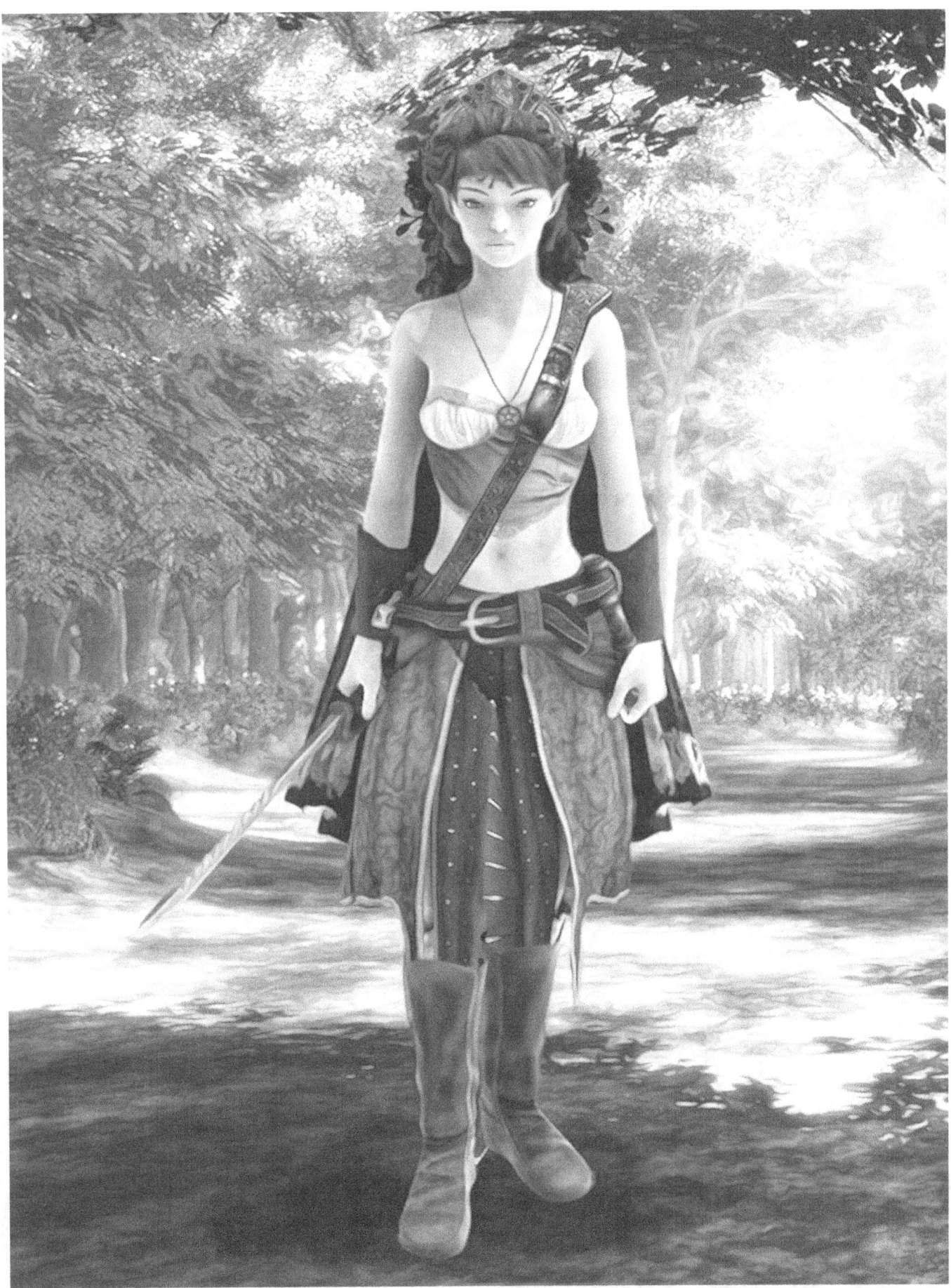

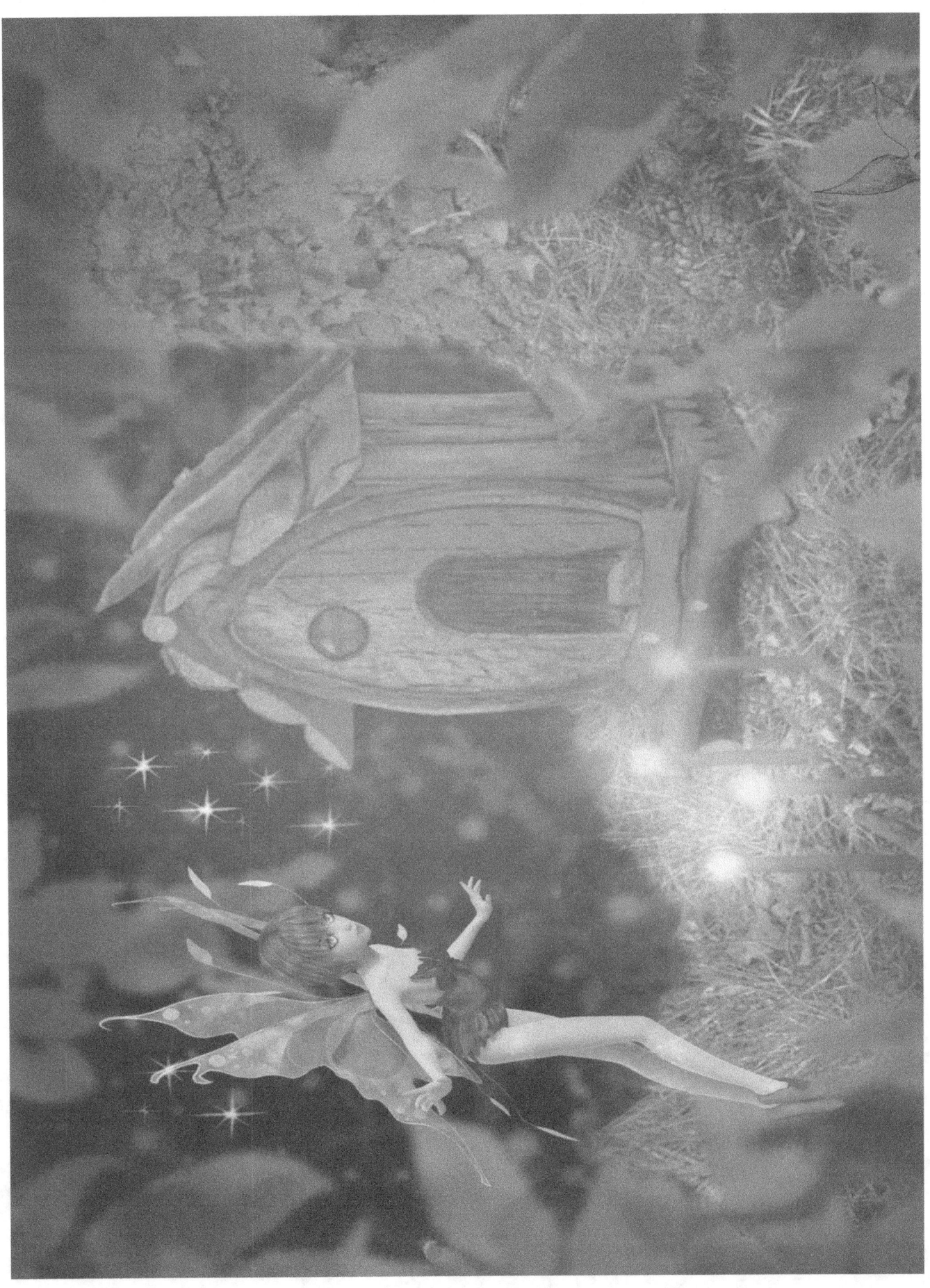

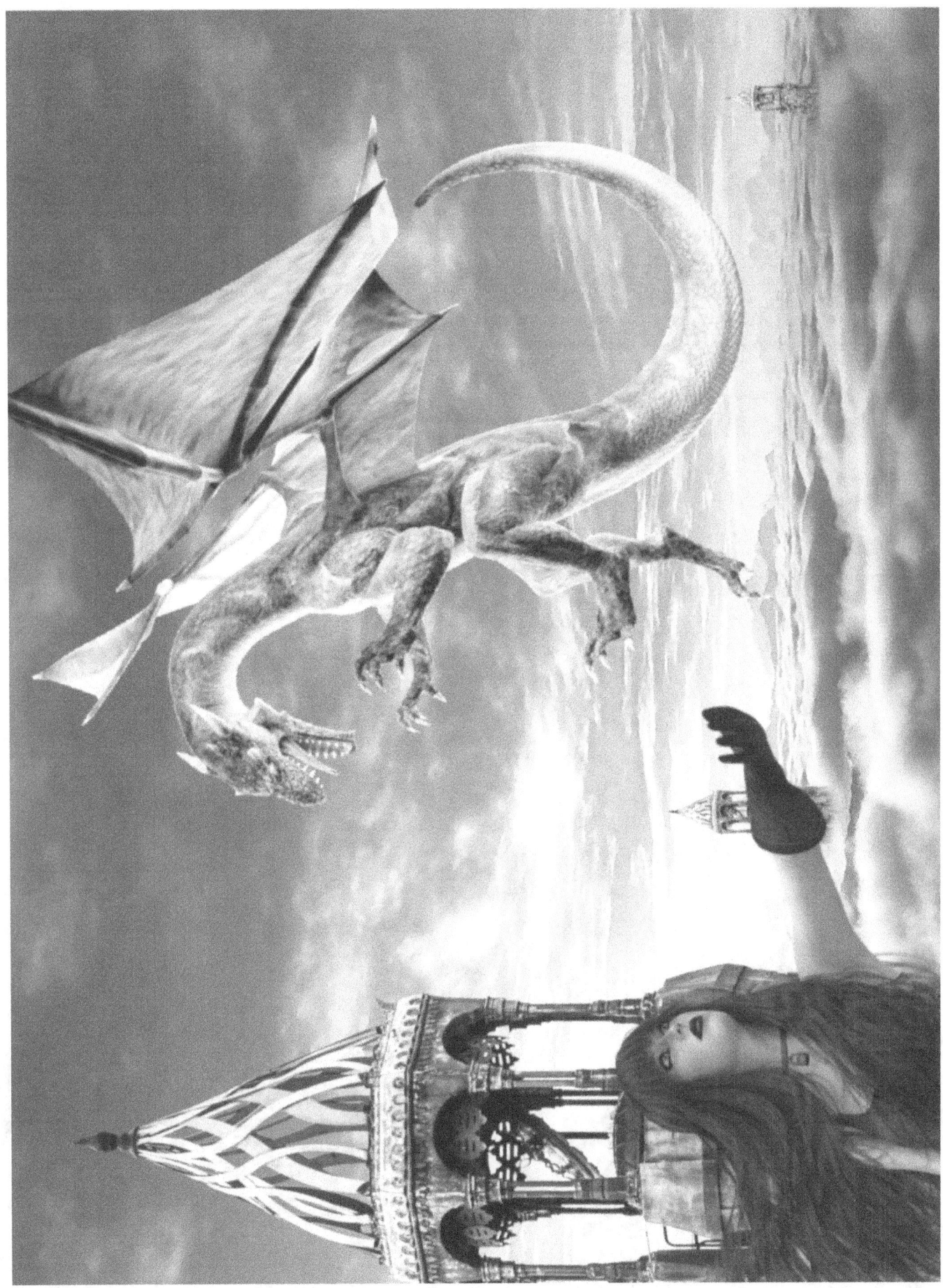

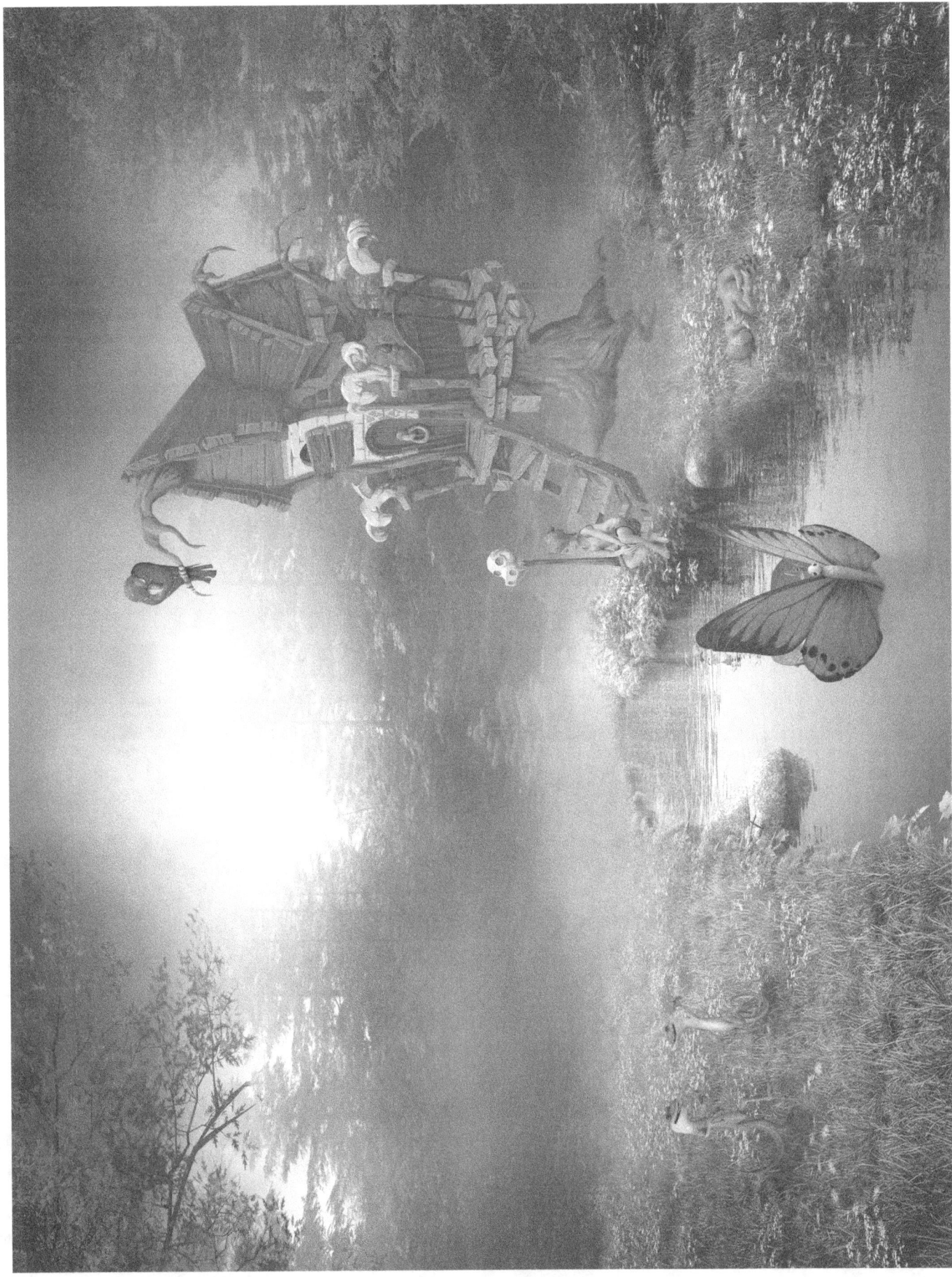

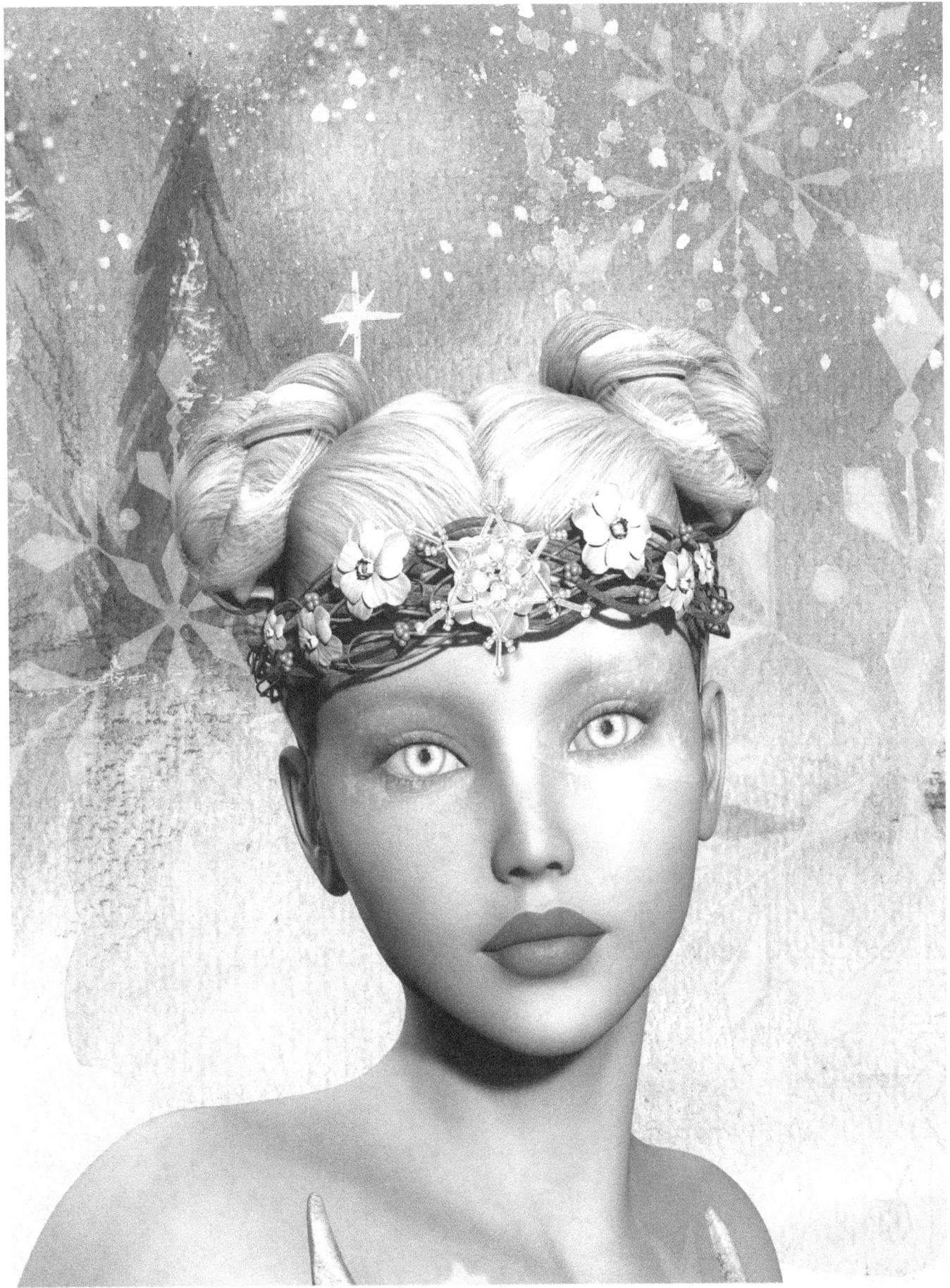

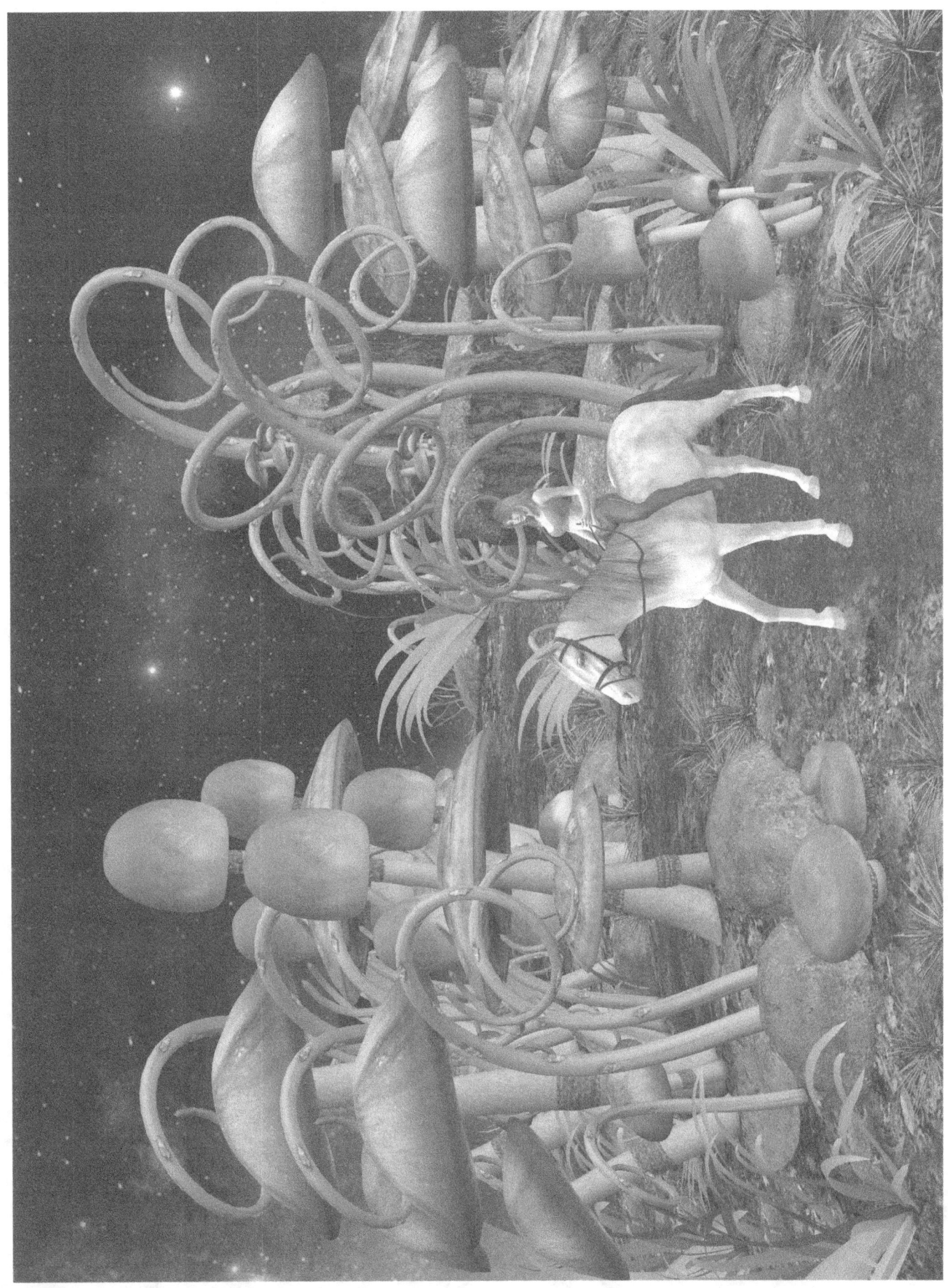

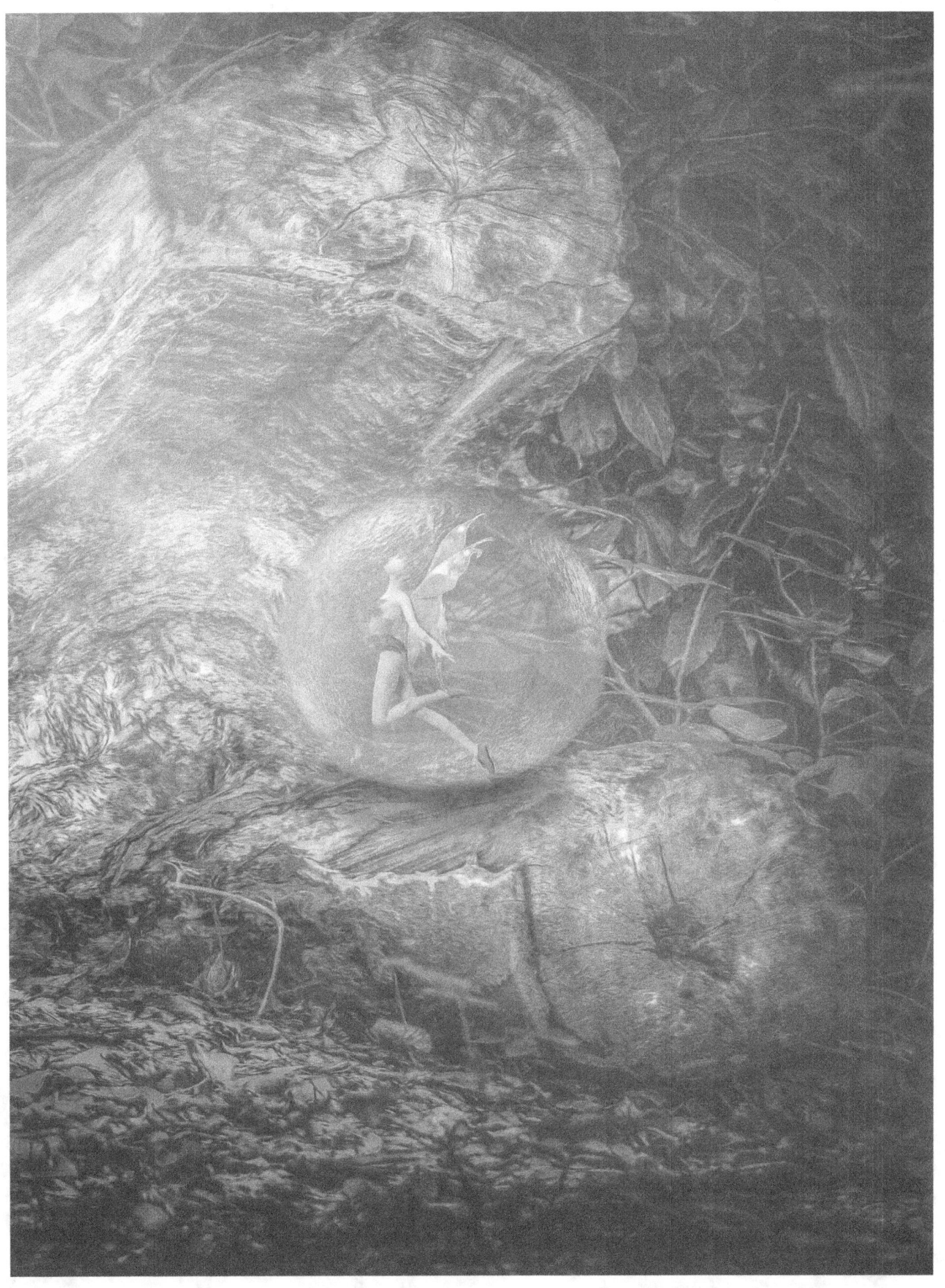

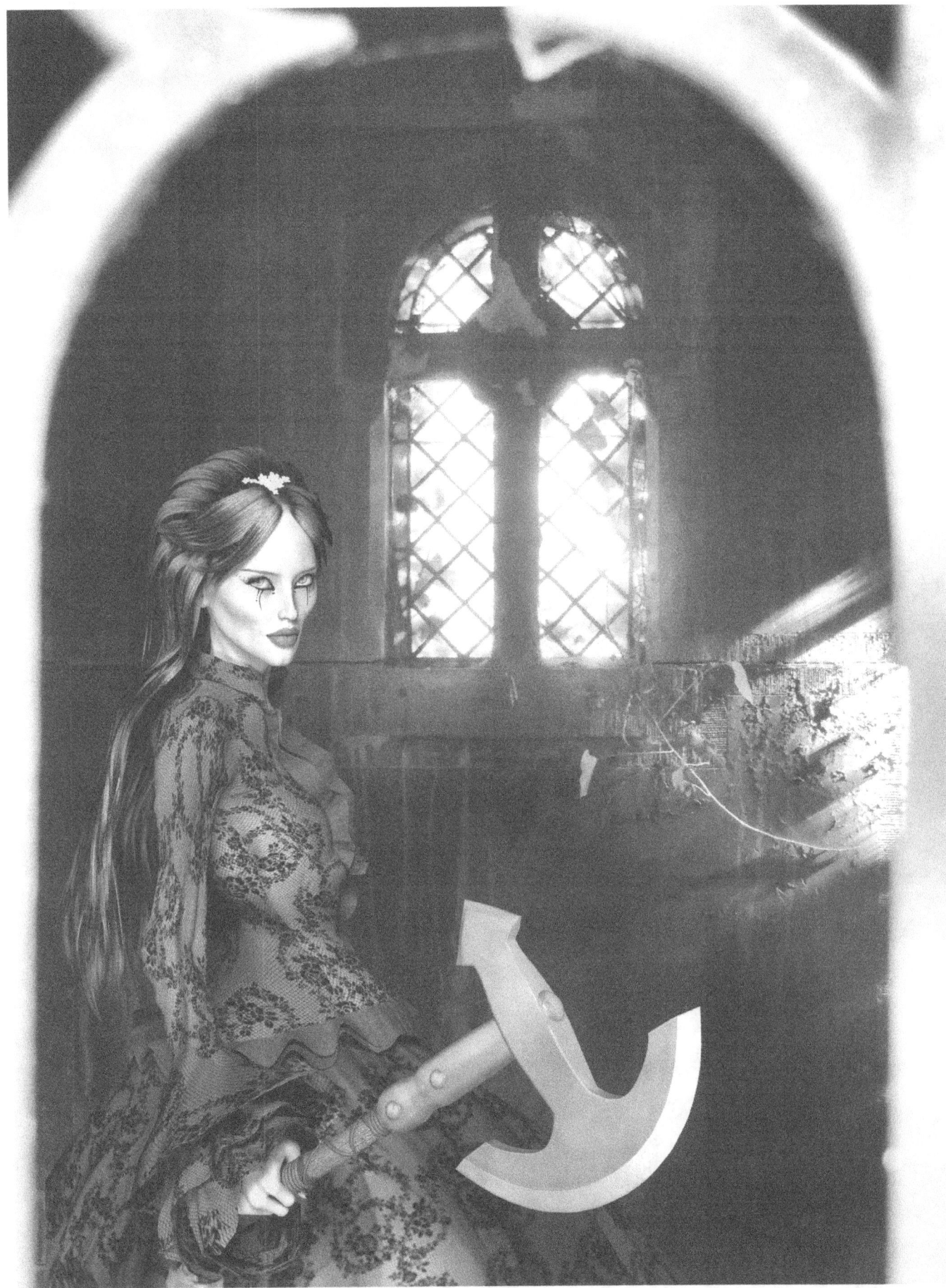

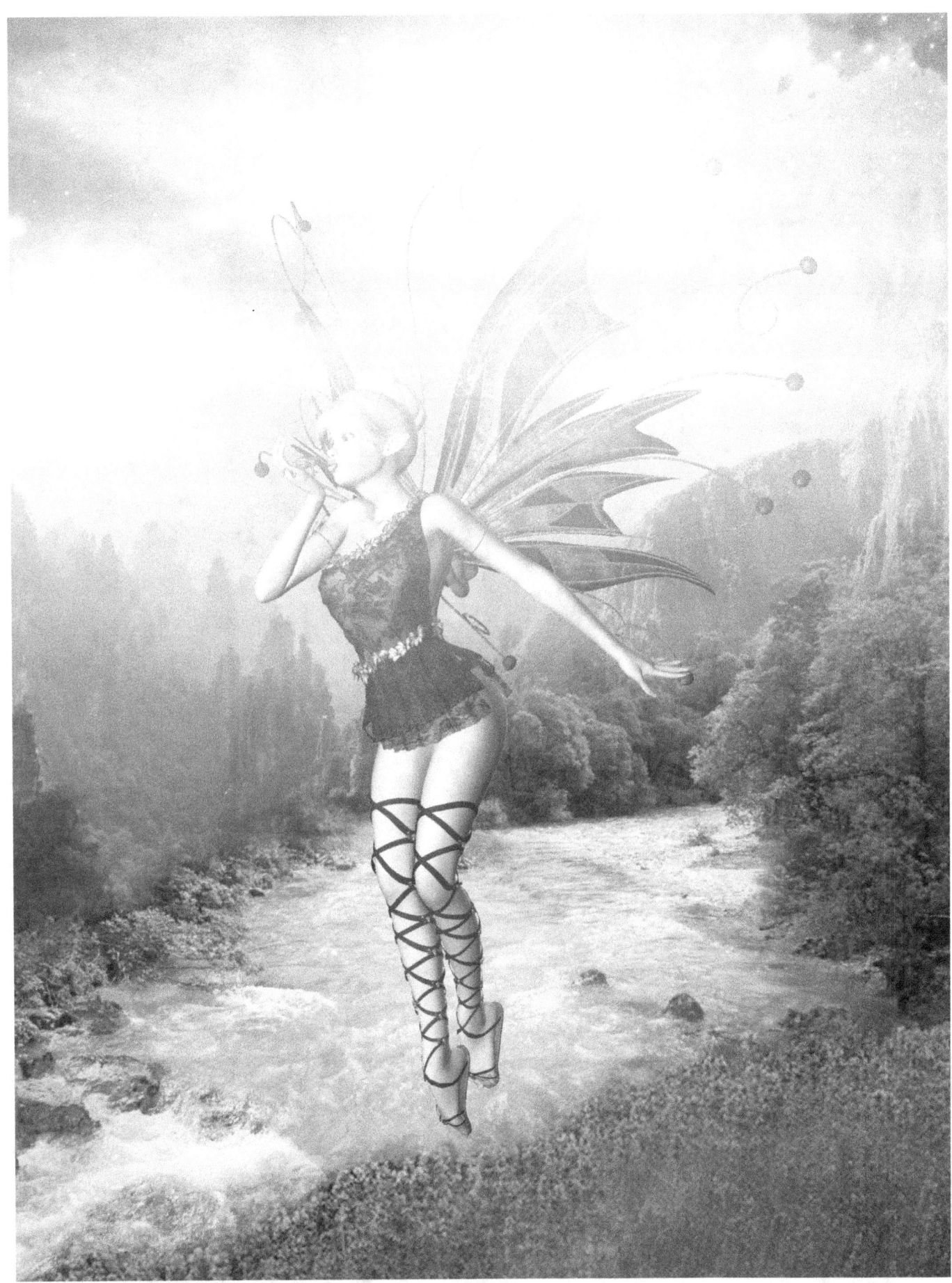

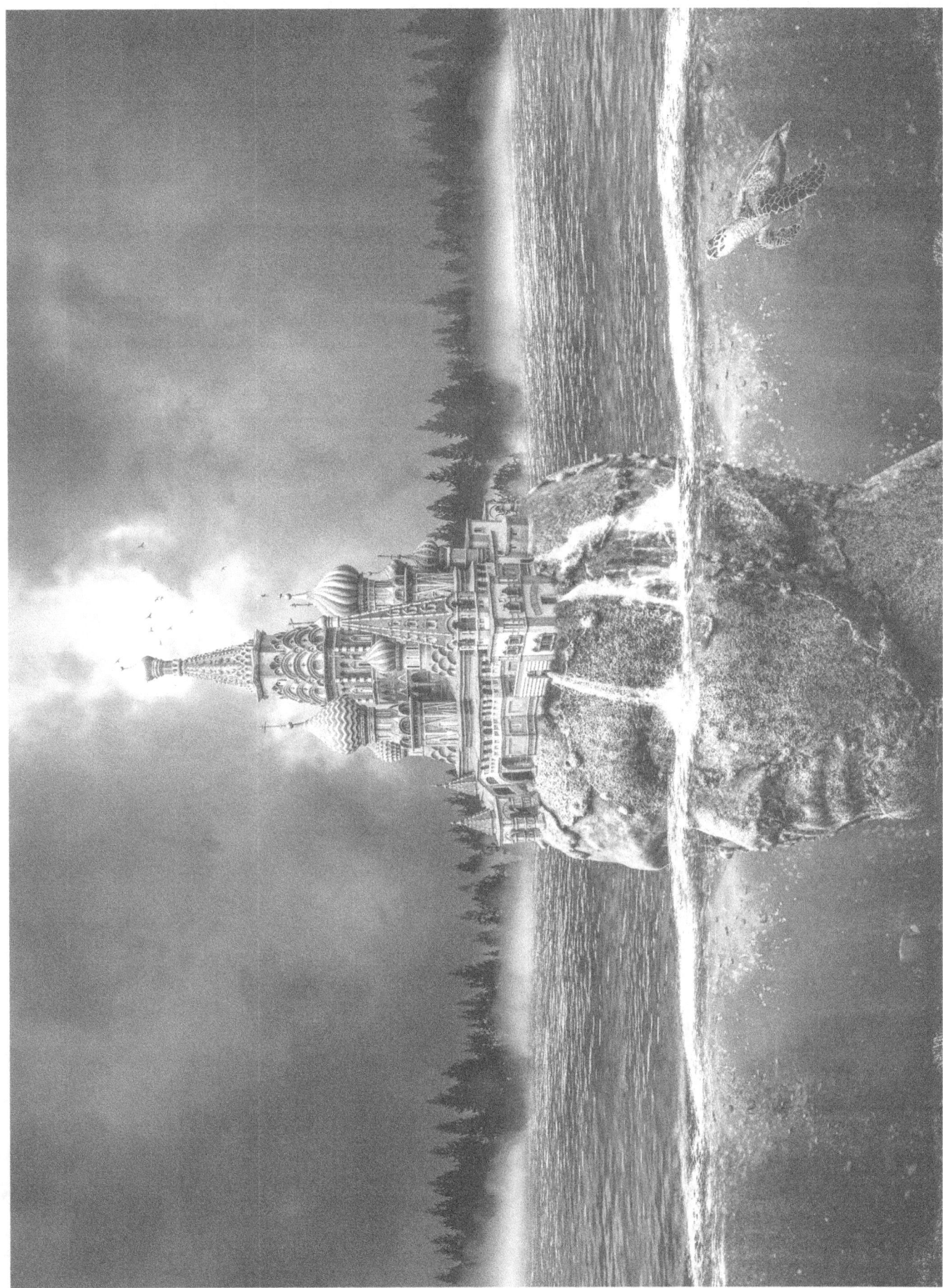

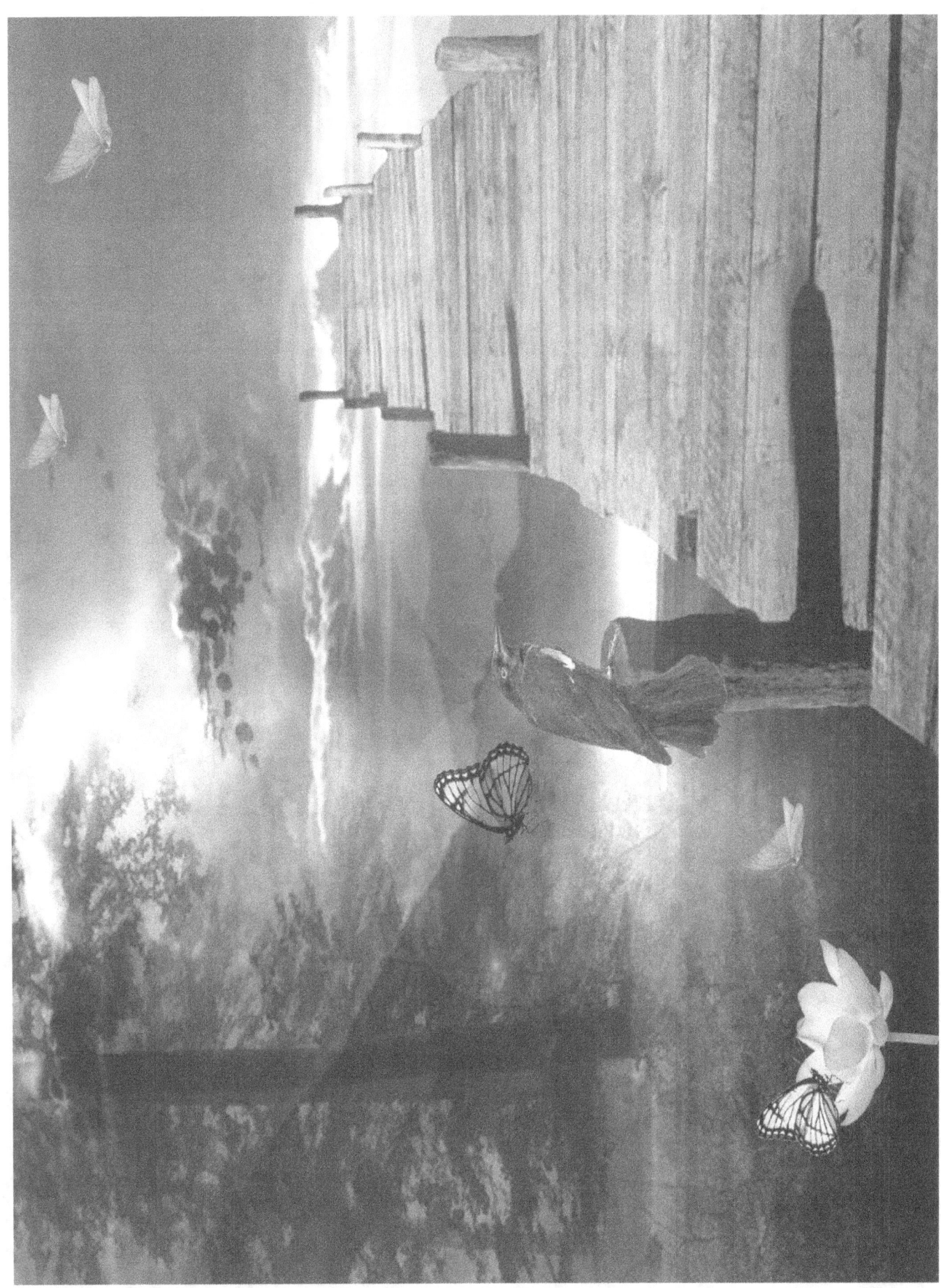

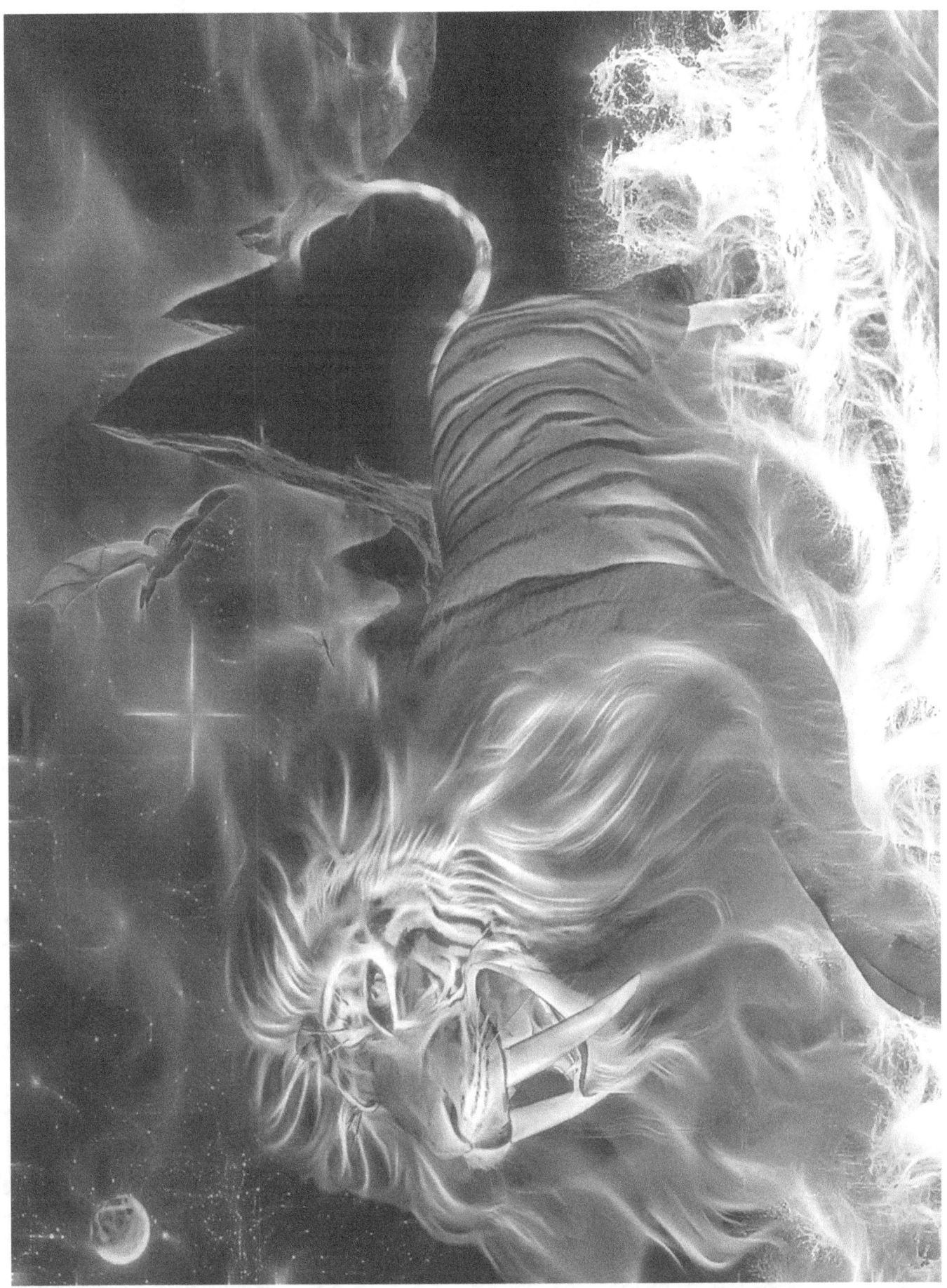

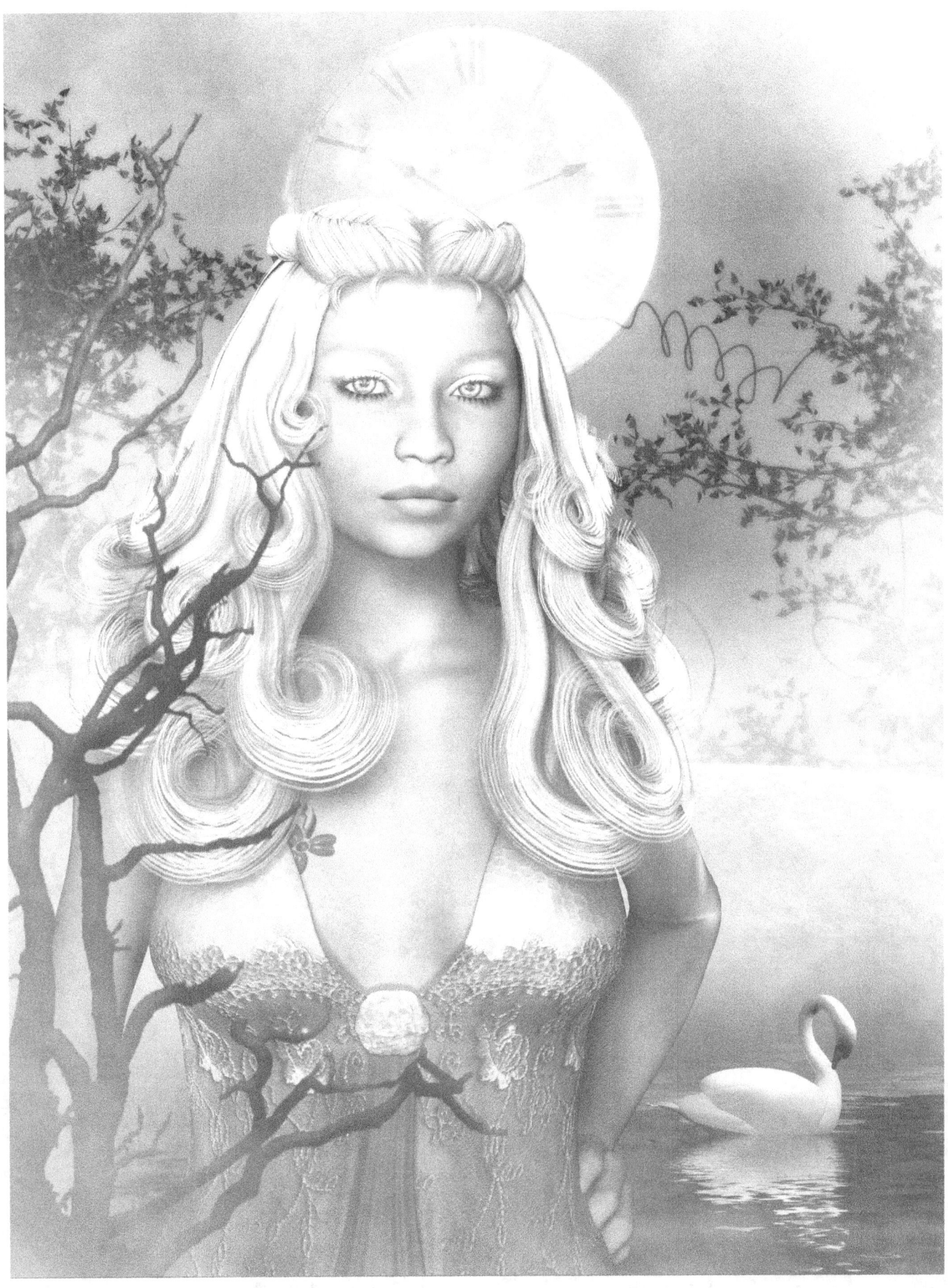

BONUS IMAGES FOR YOU TO COLOR ARE ON THE
FOLLOWING PAGES.

THANK YOU FOR PURCHASING THIS COLORING BOOK!

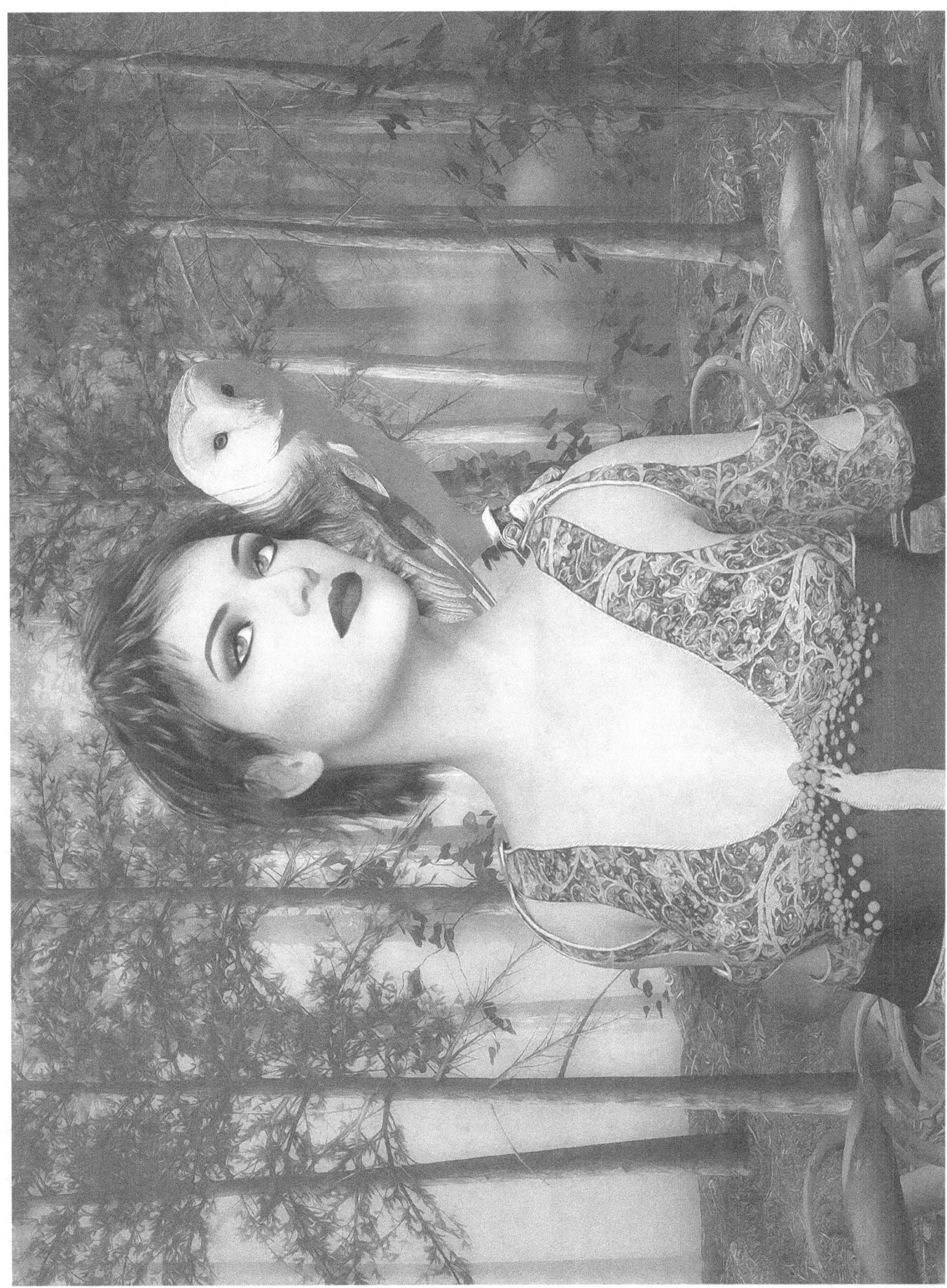

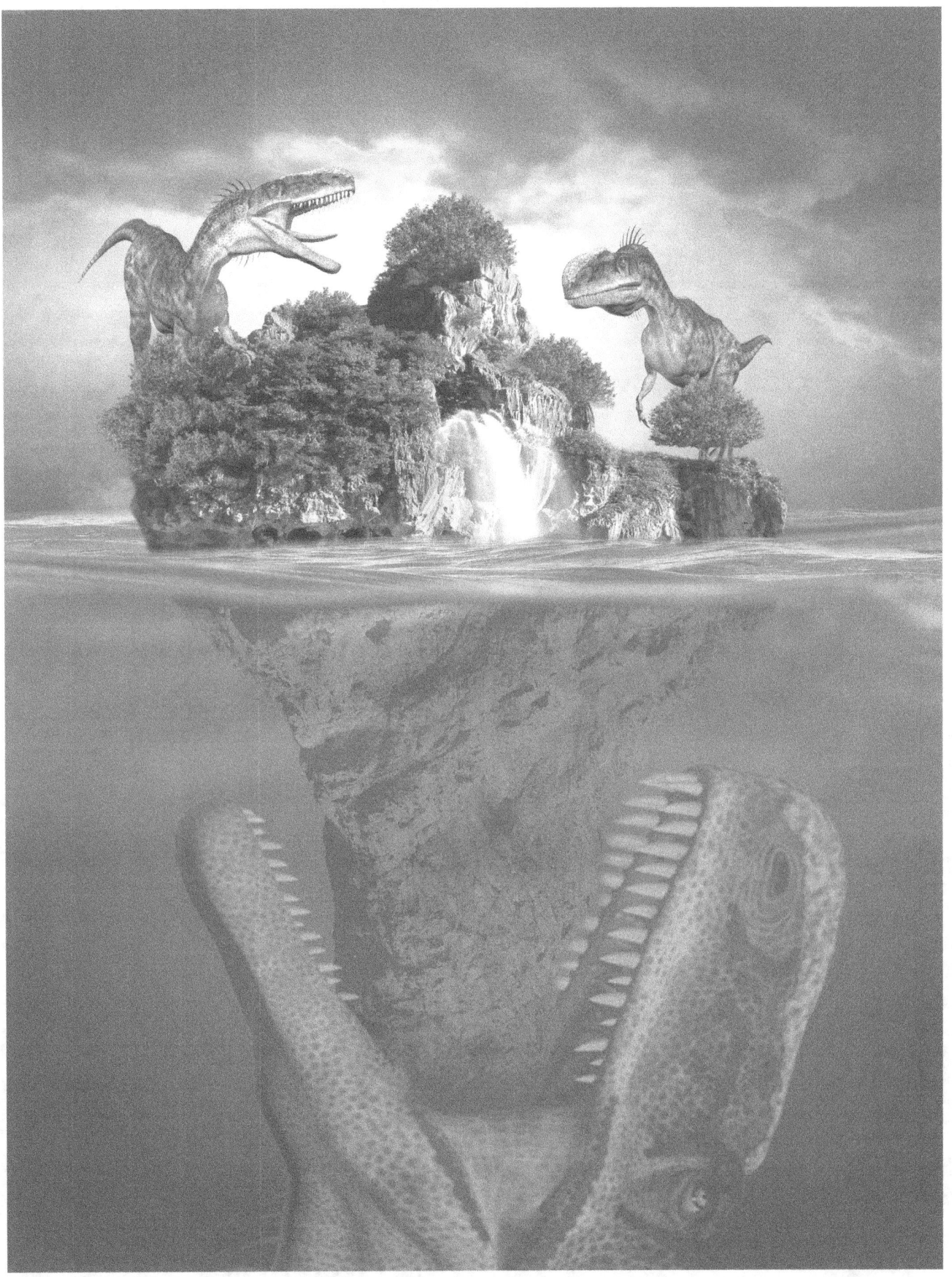

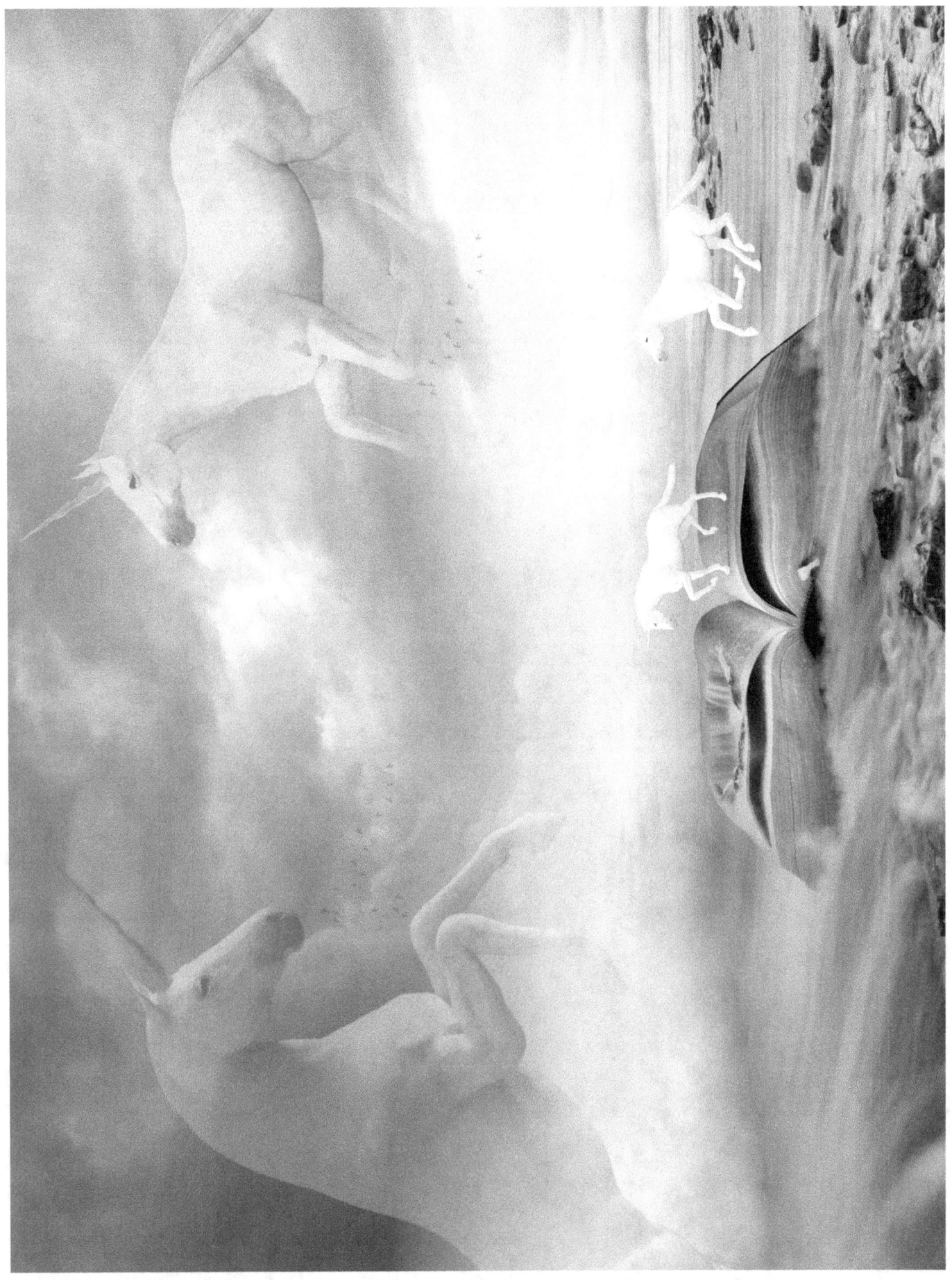

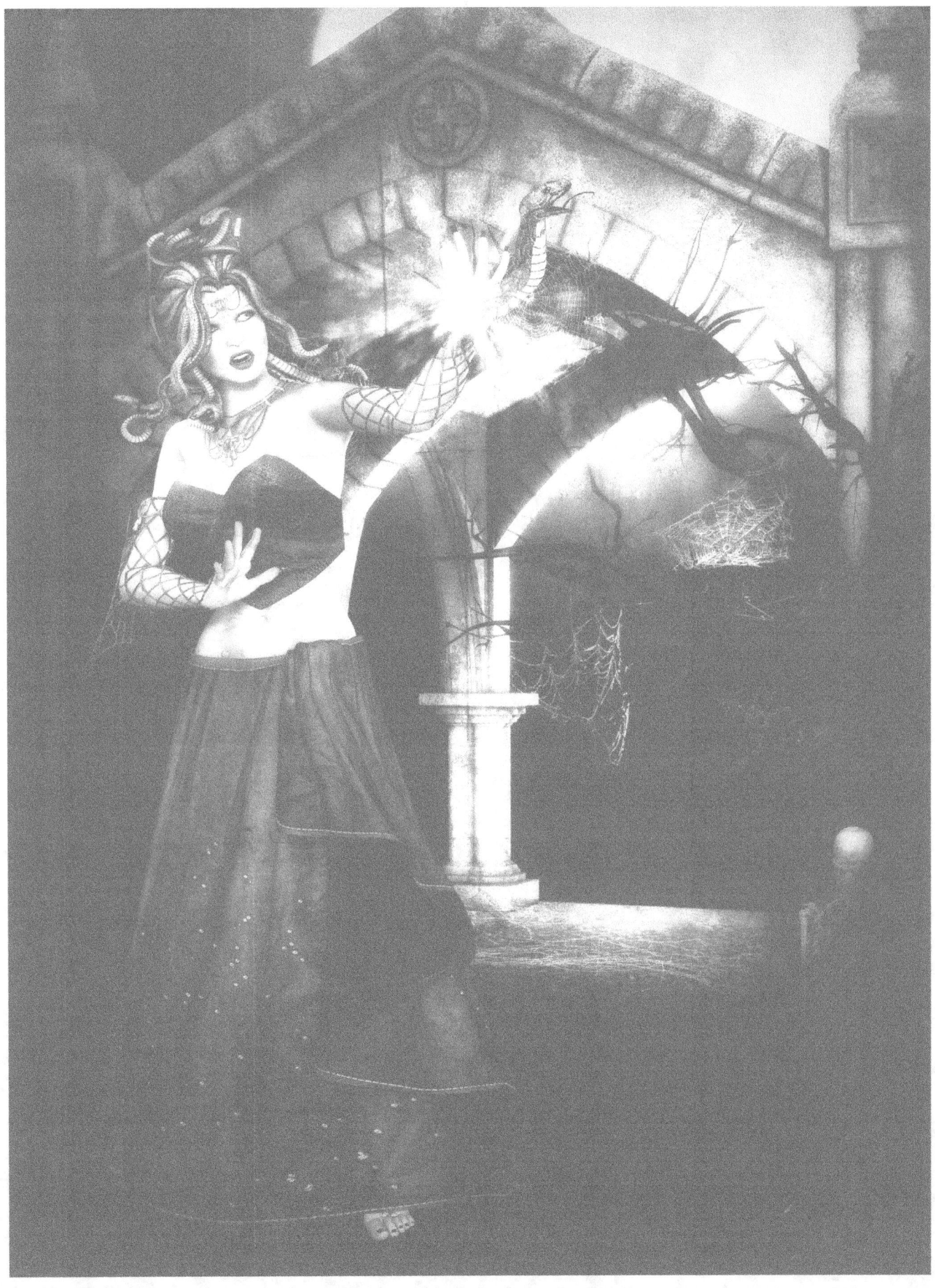

THANKS FOR PURCHASING MY BOOK!

IF YOU LIKED THIS COLORING BOOK, I WOULD POLITELY ASK IF YOU COULD GIVE A REVIEW OF IT ON AMAZON.

THANK YOU!

ABOUT THE AUTHOR

Don La Due is from the State of Washington. Don enjoys fishing, hunting and anything else that has to do with the outdoors. He creates adult coloring books and children's books when he is not writing novels.

Keep a look out for more of Don's adult coloring books on Amazon. Just do a search for Donald La Due and you will see his other books that he offers.

www.ingramcontent.com/pod-product-compliance
Lightning Source LLC
Chambersburg PA
CBHW081612200526
45167CB00019B/2811